Lore, Legends, Lies

Dr. Carolyn A. Roth

Lore, Legends, Lies

Evangelism in a multi-cultural world

CRM Publishing

Lore, Legends, Lies, Evangelism in a multi-cultural world
Copyright © 2022 by Dr. Carolyn A. Roth. All rights reserved.

Unless otherwise identified in the narrative, Scripture quotations are taken from the Holy Bible, *New International Version®*, Copyright © 1973, 1978, 1984, 2011 by Biblica, Inc. ® Used by permission of Zondervan. All rights reserved worldwide.

Published in the United States of America
Publisher: CRM Publishing

ISBN 978-1-946919-16-8
Religion
Biblical Commentary
22.09.01

I'm just a nobody trying to tell everybody about somebody who saved my soul.

— Casting Crowns, source LyricFind

ACNOWLEDGEMENTS

Pastor Myron Atkinson

Chuck Campbell for his insightful suggestions.

Bruce Roth for multiple edits.

CONTENTS

What's it About?

This central point of *Lore, Legends, Lies* is evangelism using stories from Genesis and ancient cultures. It includes truths from the *Bible*, legends, scientific thoughts, and some modern pastors' perspectives. The book even includes lies that were repeated so often that we believe them without thinking. The book points to ways evangelists can initiate conversations about Jesus as Redeemer. Importantly, *Lore, Legends, Lies* provides
information evangelists can use when responding to questions from individuals of other cultures and faiths.

Have you ever wondered why Genesis is part of the *Bible*? Increasingly, I asked myself that question. Then, it hit me! I believe Genesis is part of the *Bible* for two reasons. First, early humankind in Genesis were evangelists. It took decades of *Bible* study for me to see that. Second, Genesis shows that God is moral and just as well as loving. Each episode has a moral showing the love and justice of God, i.e., Adam expelled from the Garden of Eden, God destroying the earth in Noah's day, Abraham following God's direction to leave Haran.

We live in a multicultural world. Our neighbors may have a native American heritage or be immigrants from the Middle East (Iraq, Syria), Afghanistan, South America, or Africa. In the United States, many Latinos have cultural beliefs from indigenous peoples who lived in Middle and South America prior to arrival of Spaniards. Many Islamists are immigrants to the United States. Although the Muslim's religion developed after Christianity, Islam is now the third most practiced religion in the United States.

The Church of Jesus Christ of Latter-Day Saints (Mormons) is growing rapidly in the United States and globally. A uniquely American faith, the Mormon church eagerly shares its beliefs. Church members are intentional evangelists. Some Mormon church doctrine is included in this book; however, as with all relatively new religions, doctrine changes.

Jews are the second largest religion in the United States. At one time—about 2500 years ago and earlier—Jews were named Israelites. The Israelite/Jewish culture and religion were latecomers in the ancient near East. The ancient near East included Mesopotamia, Canaan, and Egypt.

Christianity, the majority religion on Earth, comes from the Israelite religion. Christianity is only about 2000 years old. Entire cultures and sets of spiritual beliefs developed before and after the Israelite and Christian religions developed. Often, I was unable to determine if a legend or tradition was from the Israelite or Jewish culture. For that reason, unless I am sure of the origin of the legend or tradition, I use the Israelite/Jewish descriptor.

Many cultural and religious beliefs are different from traditional Christian perspectives. Knowing alternate beliefs gives us confidence when we "go into the world and preach the gospel to every creature" (Mark

16:15); even when that world is our neighborhoods, local schools, and work settings.

In this book I don't attempt to explain all overlapping and conflicting cultural beliefs. Instead, I provide descriptions and examples of what is present. Evangelist have space to conclude how these beliefs came about, if they believe them, and how they should be used in evangelism. I've tried very hard to not criticize any culture or faith.

After evangelists learn other cultural, religious, and scientific perspectives, each has a mental file of information to pull out when discussing Christian beliefs with non-Christian colleagues.

*****

When I write episodes from Genesis, I cite *Bible* references so readers can fully read the *Bible* story. Beliefs about Islam come from the *Qur'ān*, Islamic traditions, creeds, Quranic commentaries, and "other theological writings." Christians encounter Muslims in multiple communities. Although the Church of Jesus Christ of the Latter-Day Saints, is a Christian church, I included many of their perspectives.

Many ancient beliefs described plants. When plants are named, I include the plant's taxonomy (scientific name) to assist gardeners/scholars with this key component of creation. When you see plant taxonomy names, remember that these scientific names weren't developed until the 17th and 18th centuries. Some are being clarified today.

At the end of each book chapter, is a page of study questions, named "Points to Ponder." Study questions allow readers to think deeper about chapter content and to apply answers to their lives. Study questions give ideas for personal evangelism. When you read this book and ponder study questions, don't hurry. Take time to think about viewpoints.

My personal bias is that we learn more when we study in a group or with another person. Most days my husband and I study a *Bible* passage or a topic. I don't always agree with him, however, his ideas cause me to think. Some perspectives he offers never occurred to me previously. When I think deeper about them, I can use some in my personal testimony and in my Christian world view.

*****

Recently, my pastor handed out this prayer. It speaks to evangelism.

Covenant Prayer

Pastor Myron Atkinson

Today, God, I make this covenant with you: I confess that I am no longer my own, but Yours. Help me to keep my eyes on You and never give up! Use me at work, church, home, and in the community.

Lead me to people to whom I can be an example and share my faith. Help me to think the things You want me to think. Help me to say the things You want me to say, unashamedly and with boldness.

Help me to do the things You want me to do, even if it means I am belittled, ignored, or criticized. Help me to relentless pursue You, not myself or the things of the world. Help me to relentlessly pursue the people you love. Help me to be content with nothing or much, and to use whatever I have for Your glory.

And, now God the Father, the Son, and the Holy Ghost, You are my Creator, Redeemer, and Sustainer. You are mine and I am committing to being totally Yours. Let this covenant I am making here on this Earth be acceptable and pleasing to You. Amen

1

INTRODUCTION

Cultures are filled with beliefs about creation and activities of early humankind. It's not always easy to determine which stories are true (lore), which are legends, and which are lies. Most of us don't want to believe or repeat lies. Knowing differences among lore, legends, and lies assists us to be surer about what we believe and repeat. Knowing lore, legends and lies surrounding God, creation, sin, and early humankind makes us more discerning readers and listeners. and most importantly, better evangelists.

Lore

In this book, lore is traditional knowledge or beliefs. Jews and Christians have a common set of lore which comes from the *Bible*. Jews limit their traditional beliefs to the Old Testament. Protestant Christians include the New Testament as well as the Old Testament. Catholic Christians have additional writings in the *Apocrypha*, a set of ancient writings (books), that Protestant Christians don't embrace.

Other religions have holy books and sets of beliefs. Many of these religions and cultural perspectives are admirable and are included in this text. In *Lore, Legends, Lies,* lore comes from Genesis. *Bible* content is named lore and accepted as truth.

Legends

Legends are stories that come from the past, handed down from generation to generation. Other names for legends are myths and fables. Most legends can't be proven or disproven. Ancient peoples used legends to explain the unexplainable, i.e., presence of humans on Earth.

At one time many legends were considered accurate by individuals who repeated them. With advances in science and religious scholarship, some legends were fully or partially disproven. Still, they remain in the culture. Fables include a moral or principle for living life. Perhaps, a fable remains in a culture because of its excellent moral for life.

Different cultures have different legends. In those cultures individuals value stories and legends as much as Americans value stories and legends of their culture. Did Johnny Appleseed cross the United States planting apple seeds? Did Washington say, "I cannot tell a lie"?

Frequently, legends from different cultures have common elements. Many anthropologist and Christian scholars believe that a story, or part of a story, from one culture was incorporated into another culture's legends. For example, lore from the *Bible* included legends from other cultures. Other cultures could include *Bible* stories.

Some Americans believe certain *Bible* stories are legends. At a church event, a woman told me that the *Bible* story of Jonah swallowed by a whale was a legend put in the *Bible* to illustrate a moral principle. I gave no response. I simply don't know if this *Bible* story is or isn't a legend. My rational mind says that it could be a legend. At the same time, I believe the *Bible* is true. Some modern *Bible* scholars name Jonah the first missionary in the *Bible*.

Many scientist have elaborate theories of how things came to be and work. Some scientific theories are true. Others were disproven, i.e. why plants have thorns and thistles. Present-day scientific theories may be future legends.

The *Bible* includes superstitious beliefs that characters in Genesis practiced. A superstitions is a misconception, or a fantasy, that individuals believe. It's folklore. I am putting superstitions under legends because some can't be proven or disproven. Most are false, for example, finding a four-leaf clover resulting in good luck.

Lies

Lies occur when a person creates a false and misleading impression. In the first quarter of the 21st century, Americans encounter lies in news stories, on social media, in scientific assertions, and pastor's sermons. Often, media attempt to sanitize these lies by calling them "spin" or "disinformation." Spin occurs when partial truths, or selective data, are put forth as accurate and complete. The purpose of spin is to deceive. In the Garden of Eden, Satan deceived the first humans into disobeying God.

In the past two centuries in western society, science assumed the role legends occupied in ancient cultures. Scientific theories of creation and humankind are the lore, legends, and lies of 19th-21st century individuals.

Like legends, scientific proposals often can't be proven or disproven. We repeat scientific explanations as if they were 100% accurate. That's not always correct. Imagine 23rd century scientists looking back on science of the 21st century. Much 21st century science will be disproven by the 23rd century.

Many of us read commentaries from theologians we admire. We listen intently to pastors' sermons. Theologians including pastors provide insights that never occurred to us. However, pastors' sermons can go beyond *Bible* statements. Sometimes their proposals and content can't be proven or disproven, just like some legends can't be proven or disproven.

What about Evangelism?

Go into all the world (even just next door) and tell individuals about the redeeming power of Jesus.

Definitions of evangelism that resonate with me are "enthusiastic proponent" and "zealous advocate for a cause." Think about these words! Are you an enthusiastic proponent for God? Do you advocate for God's cause? Evangelism is telling others what Jesus did in your life. Evangelism is advocating for Jesus.

Individuals must believe before they act, that is, before they are an enthusiastic proponent or zealous advocate. Belief precedes actions. What or who we believe in has our allegiance. God should have a Christian's enthusiastic allegiance. Does God have your allegiance? God has to be more important than a political party, a nation, a race, family members, etc.

What does a Christian evangelist need to believe in or about? In the second decade of the 21st century, it seems like Christian belief is a moving target. Some individuals who name themselves "Christians" believe one thing, while others believe something else entirely.

Under this section on evangelism, I'm not going to discuss what a mature, sanctified Christian looks like or needs to know. Rather, I am going to list the minimum requirements for an evangelist to believe and teach when sharing the good news of Jesus' redemption. This is my list. Admittedly, others many have an alternative list.

1. God is Creator and Sustainer of the cosmos and planet Earth.
2. Jesus Christ is God's son.
3. The first humankind rebelled (sinned) against God and all humankind thereafter sinned (rebelled against God).
4. Jesus was born of the Virgin Mary. Jesus is fully man through his mother Mary and fully God through God's spirit coming on Mary to conceive Jesus.
5. While Jesus lived on earth, he taught and performed miracles. He was sinless.
6. Jesus was crucified, died on a cross, and buried.

7. Jesus rose from the grave, lived on earth another 40 days, then went to live with God.
8. To live eternally in Heaven, an individual must accept Jesus as the Savior of his/her life.

My allegiance is to the Triune God — Father, Son (Jesus the Christ), and Holy Spirit. I try to know God at an increasingly deeper level. I read the *Bible*, attend *Bible* studies, pray, etc. What about you? Do you attempt to know God who you say has your allegiance?

After identifying who has his/her allegiance, an evangelist must listen. Recently, my husband's brother and wife visited. They are members of the Church of Jesus Christ of the Latter-Day Saints. They hold different beliefs than we do. For the first time (in 30 years), we listened to them. We listened not to criticize their beliefs but to build a relationship with them. While building a relationship, we heard each other's ideas, perspectives, and beliefs.

A step of evangelization is formulating a personal testimony. People love stories. What is your story? What has God done for you? As you probably know, I write books. Publishing gurus advise authors to have a 2-3-minute synopsis of their book to pitch to potential publishers they meet at writer's conferences. This synopsis is named an "elevator pitch." It should last no longer than an elevator trip up or down.

I don't think that evangelists need to limit their personal testimony to three minutes. At the same time, unless your story is particularly compelling, target audiences stop listening after 5-8 minutes. Tell targets your story, then, give them an opportunity to ask questions about it. If you don't get questions back, perhaps your target isn't listening. Consider recrafting your testimony.

I am never going to Africa or South America as an evangelist. I'm going to live my life is southwestern Virginia. That doesn't mean that I'm not an evangelist. My surrounding communities — rather than off-shore communities — are my evangelism fields. Individuals living in these communities are the targets of my evangelism efforts, i.e., family members, neighbors, church congregates, social clubs, etc. In other words, individuals I have contact with.

Many Christian evangelists ask, "Why should I bother learning what is true, legend, or downright lies about episodes in the *Bible*?" My personal answer is so that you accurately tell others (evangelize) about the Triune God. Plus, so evangelists respond accurately when others push back on their words and actions. That's another point, expect pushback and prepare for it.

This morning Bruce (my husband) and I discussed when do we know enough to start evangelizing, telling others about Jesus. We concluded that if we wait until we knew everything about God and contrasting cultural beliefs, we will never tell others about God. We will never know all there is to know. At the same time, I'm not sure (and I am willing to admit that I could be wrong) that an individual can come to a saving knowledge of Jesus Christ one day and begin evangelizing the next day. There needs to be space to grow in deeper knowledge of Jesus' teachings. Some call this sanctification. I think of it as moving from drinking milk to eating meat (Hebrews 5:11-14).

Bruce is suspicious about lists, steps, and using acronyms to pray and study the *Bible*. I'm an educator and like techniques, steps, outlines, etc. So here's my list for how to evangelize:

1. Know in whom you believe. A Christian evangelists believes in the Triune God.
2. Listen first, speak second. Build a relationship before you attempt to evangelize a person.
3. Give a short personal testimony (your story). You don't need to "wow" your target with all you know about God.
4. Be willing to admit when you don't know something. At the same time, continually study so that you have an answer when individuals challenge expressions of your faith.
5. After an individual accepts Jesus as their Redeemer, assist him/her to find a church where he/she can be discipled in the faith. Don't drop your interest in the person.

I believe that the evangelist and discplier (is this a word?) usually aren't the same person. Discipling a person takes time — even years. I tend to be the evangelist in my family, while Bruce is the discipler.

*****

Scientists, *Bible* scholars, and pastors have proposed multiple explanations for *Bible* events. At times these explanations cause individuals to reject *Bible* truths, claiming that Christianity is "so confusing."

As a researcher and educator, I read and listen to alternative points of view. At the same time, I don't accept them without careful assessment and evaluation. I go back to the *Bible*; that is my truth (lore). I remember that current opinions of scientists and pastors could be wrong, just as some legends of ancient peoples were wrong. At one time, individuals believed that the world was flat. If a ship sailed west far enough, the ship would fall off the Earth. In the Middle Ages, astrologists believed that the Earth was the center of the universe.

What about you — what is your mind set when you read social media, watch videos and the evening news, and listen to sermons? How does the information you read and hear compare with truth? Do you ponder each piece of information critically or believe all input? Bruce received a telephone call from a loyal member of the church. She asked if she should believe every portion of the pastor's sermon. Bruce said, "No." In the 21st century, congregates must verify even Sunday sermons with the Word of God.

Points to Ponder

1. Americans live in a pluralistic society. What does that even mean? Are their implications for evangelism because of the society we live in?

2. If you want to be an evangelist, why do you need to differentiate among lore, legends, and lies?

3. Are there any American folktales (legends) that are likely false? Relate one. How could it be true? How could it be false?

4. How should each — lore, legends, lies — be used as you evangelize your communities? Or, perhaps, you shouldn't use legends and lies in your evangelism.

5. Have you ever repeated an elaborate story that you believed? Later, you learned the story was a lie. How do you feel about yourself for believing the tale? How do you feel about the source, the person who told you the story?

6. Craft your personal testimony of what Jesus did for you.

SECTION A
IN THE BEGINNING

Is Genesis chapters 1-11 an allegory, a legend written by the Israelite/Jewish community to account for creation of the Earth and sin entering the world? Is the *Bible* story of Noah's flood a legend? Some individuals, including noted clergy, believe they are.

In contrast, other individuals believe the unfolding of creation outlined in Genesis 1-11 is an accurate depiction of God's act of creation. Several days ago I posted the following question on social media: "Do any of you believe that God created the Earth in six (24 hour) days." I received many responses, 90% of which were "Yes," with the caveat that six days wasn't necessarily a 24-hour period as we know it today.

Section A helps you discern what you believe by giving lore, legends, and lies from the *Bible* from cultures other than Christian culture. It includes six chapters. First, I present some creation legends from a variety of ancient cultures and from 1-2 present-day religions. Second, I drill down on legends about the first humankind. Stories about sin entering creation is the next chapter. The fourth and fifth chapters are about the Deluge (flood) of Noah's time and subsequent devolution of society.

Section A's purpose isn't to debate whether the first eleven chapters of Genesis is poetry, parable, legend, or truth. Greater minds than mine have explored these issue over millennia. Instead, I name the first eleven Genesis chapters "lore" or truth. Then, identify how *Bible* lore describes individuals' interactions with each other, with their environments, and with their Creator. I compare and contrast *Bible* lore with legends that existed before, during, and after the *Bible*'s description of God's creation.

Don't neglect to read these legends, even lies. They help you to be a better listener to others' points of view, particularly non-Christian's viewpoints. Listening, rather, than speaking, is a beginning step in evangelization.

Plants were central to lives of ancient humans, more central than they are to humankind's life in the 21st century. Plants grow and reproduce just like humans grow and reproduce; however, plants differ from humans and animals. God never breathed into plants the breath of life as he did into humans and animals. Despite this major difference between man and plants, early humankind developed legends and lies about plants. Ancient individuals gave plants human attributes.

2

CREATION, PARADISE

Most cultures identified that water was present at the start of creation. All else in creation came after or from water. Usually, a deity or deities acted on the water as a step in the creation process. As you read early creation stories below, look for similarities between your faith's creation story and that of other cultures.

Water, Water Everywhere

The area between the Tigris and Euphrates Rivers is named the "Cradle of Civilization," or <u>Mesopotamia</u>. Most scientists believe that human life originated there. Primarily, three early civilizations flourished in Mesopotamia in ancient times — Sumer in the south, Akkad north of Sumer, and Assyria north of Akkad. Mesopotamia was a thriving area thousands of years before 2000 BCE, the earliest date proposed for Israelite Patriarchs.

One of the oldest and arguably best-known <u>Mesopotamian</u> creation stories was *The Seven Tablets of Creation,* commonly called the *Enuma Elish.* The *Enuma Elish* proposed that in the beginning there was only undifferentiated water, swirling in chaos. The first creation activity was separation of the undifferentiated water into fresh (a god, Apsu) and salt (a goddess, Tiamat) water. No entity caused this water separation; it just happened. From the union of

Apsu and Tiamat came younger gods. One was Marduk. Marduk and a fellow god created humans to help gods maintain order, keep chaos at bay, and served gods, especially providing them food.

The Yoruba's (Nigeria, Africa), home to many African people who were enslaved in the United States, creation story is that Truth (a deity) was sent to a newly formed earth to determine if humans could live there. Truth found that the earth was too wet. Yoruban gods made the earth's crust dry and fertile so it supported human, animal, and plant life.

In Islam, Allah existed alone in eternity. Then, Allah created the heavens and earth from nothing (*ex nihilo*). Allah spoke the heavens and earth into existence. Classic Islam has no reference to primordial water as in many belief systems. The creation story found in the *Bible* is largely accepted in Islam, Judaism, and Christianity.

Mormons believe that God created the world out of substances already present but not necessarily water. Further, Latter-Day Saints' doctrine teaches that God created other worlds as well as Earth. Likely, the other worlds were created from a primal substance also.

The *Bible* recorded that in the beginning, the earth was covered by water. After God created the earth, God created plants, animals, and celestial bodies. Christians believe that God created through his Son (the *Logos*), Jesus, the Christ. God created the earth from nothing.

Utopias and Afterlife

Most cultures postulated a utopian place where nature and beauty abounded. Individuals could enter utopia after they died. Greek mythology named this place of perfection "Elysium, Isle of the Blessed." Individuals went there if they lived a good life. There, they didn't work. Nor was there trouble or conflict. Honey-sweet fruit from trees nourished the blessed who lived in Elysium.

Ancient Celts (mostly Irish) believed that an earthly Paradise existed on the enchanted Isle of Avalon — the Island of the Blest — described in the following poem:

> Where falls not hail or rain, or any snow,
> Nor even wind blows loudly; but it lies
> Deep-meadow'd, happy, fair, with
> Orchard lawn and bowery hollows.

In Mexico, Aztec native people postulated that after death all mortals went to Mictlan. If certain conditions were met, the soul traveled to Tlalocan, a place of peace, filled with flowers and dancing. Four giant trees held up the top of Tlalocan.

In the Americas not all indigenous people included utopias in belief systems. For example, Cherokee natives of North America believed that when ancestors died they entered a cedar tree (see the scroll on the next page). After you read beliefs and activities of Cherokee people, compare their use of cedar wood with Christian's use of a cross/crucifix.

Ancestor Spirits

A Cherokee Legend

The Cherokee believe that the spirits of ancestors live in cedar trees (*Cedrus libani*).

When Cherokees smell the aroma of the cedar tree or gaze upon the tree, they remember that they are looking on Cherokee ancestors.

The wood of the cedar tree holds powerful protective spirits for the Cherokee. Some Cherokees carry a small piece of cedar wood in a medicine bag worn around the neck.

A traditional Cherokee drum used to call ancestors is made from cedar wood.

Cedar is placed above entrances to houses so ancestors can protect inhabitants against entry of evil spirits.

In the ancient <u>Sumerian</u> (part of <u>Mesopotamia</u>) culture, only gods lived in utopias. After a human died, his/her soul went to Kur (Irkalla). Kur was a dark, dreary cavern located deep below the surface of the earth. There, inhabitants continued a shadowy version of life on earth. All human souls went to the same afterlife. A person's actions during life had no effect on how the person was treated in the world to come. When I read about Kur, I thought about my girlhood vision of Hell/Hades.

<u>Muslims</u> call their paradise Jannah. In the *Qur'ān*. Jannah is described as a beautiful garden. Muslims go to Jannah if they lived a good life. Jahannam is where Muslims who lived a bad life, or a life contrary to Allah's teachings, go after death. Jahannam is a place of fire and torment, a place of physical and spiritual suffering. Jahannam sounds similar to the Judeo-Christian belief of Hell, a place of physical torment. Also, Jahannam echoes Sumerian Kur (Irkalla).

<u>Mormons</u> believe in an afterlife. Evil individuals and those who totally reject God go to a place of eternal torment (Hell), separated from God. A unique point of view of Mormons is belief in three levels of glory which are assigned after God judges individuals. The highest is the Celestial Kingdom. The lowest is the Telestial Kingdom. The middle is the Terrestrial Kingdom. Assignment to a kingdom is based on an individual's belief in Jesus' atonement and his/her behavior on Earth. To me this seems like different levels of Heaven. Initially, levels of heaven seemed strange to me, then I remembered the *Bible* alludes to them (2 Corinthians 12:2)

The *Bible* named a utopian-like place the "Garden of Eden." Judeo-Christians believe that God placed the first created humans in the Garden of Eden. Below is a description of the Garden of Eden from Genesis:

> The Lord God had planted a garden in the east, in Eden; and there he put the man he had formed. The Lord God made all kinds of trees grow out of the ground—trees that were pleasing to the eye and good for food. In the middle of the garden were the tree of life and the tree of the knowledge of good and evil. A river watering the garden flowed from Eden (Genesis 2:8-10).

Most *Bible* scholars located the Garden of Eden in Mesopotamia where the Tigris and Euphrates Rivers came together near the Persian Gulf. As late as 1552 CE, a region in Mesopotamia was named "Eden." Other legends postulated that the Garden of Eden was near Mount Lebanon in Syria or in Armenia. Some Jewish scholars contend that the Garden of Eden is at Jerusalem. Mormons believe that after the second coming of Jesus, Earth will be reconfigured and the Garden of Eden will be in the United States.

Trees in Creation

Creation legends describe sacred or supernatural plants, mostly trees. In the Mayan (Central America) culture, heaven is named Tomaoanchan. Heaven is a mystical mountain on Earth which contains the World Tree. At the base of the World Tree, flows all layers of existence, i.e., heaven, earth, underworld.

On the next page is a creation legend from <u>Korea</u> that has a tree at the center. In this legend, humankind came from a giant cinnamon tree. Notice the Korean legend only describes the creation of a man, not a man and a woman.

Many cultures have beliefs about a tree that gives life. <u>Hindus</u> believe the banyan tree (*Ficus benghalensis*) is the tree of life. During a destruction of creation when the earth was enveloped by waters, the banyan tree remained unaffected. Buddha meditates eternally under the banyan tree. I marvel that *Ficus* tree species played such a seminal role in Christianity, Judaism, and Hinduism.

<u>Chinese</u> mythology posits that the tree of life is a peach tree (*Prunus persica*). The tree produces a peach every 3000 years. The person who eats the fruit becomes immortal. If the tree only produces a peach every 3000 years, immortality is rare.

A variety of trees grew in the Garden of Eden (*Bible*). Two were singled out with names: the tree of knowledge of good and evil and the tree of life. In Noah's time a flood ended the known world. The topography (landscape, geography, structure, scenery) of Earth was obliterated and remade (Genesis 7:11, 19-23). I surmise that the Garden of Eden was destroyed along with its trees.

Genesis includes information on the importance of the tree of knowledge of good and evil. In this book the information is included in chapters on Adam and Eve (Chapter 3) and Sin Enters Creation (Chapter 4).

Origin of First Man

A Korean Legend

A giant cinnamon tree (*Cinnamomum verum* AKA *C. zeylanicum*) was the only tree on earth. Fairies came from heaven to rest in its shade. No one knew how old the tree was; it grew larger and larger.

When the wind blew, a fairy felt the tree's movement. She came down from heaven in response to its call.

Once when the fairy was nestled in the arms of the giant tree, she conceived a son.

When the boy was 7 years-old, the fairy returned to heaven. The son grew in the tender care of his tree-father.

After a long time the cinnamon tree died; however, the son lived. He was the first man.

Tree of Life

Not until the final *Bible* book (Revelations) do readers learn what ultimately happened to the tree of life that was in the Garden of Eden. Revelations (chapter 21 and 22) describes a future world (Heaven) accessible to believers in Jesus, Son of God. The Christian Heaven is named New Jerusalem (Revelation 22:1-3). In New Jerusalem, a river flows down a street from the throne of God. Tree of life are on both sides of the street. Tree of life produce fruit each month. Fruit are available for individuals in New Jerusalem to eat. The *Bible* remains silent on the tree's species and type of fruit.

What about Evangelism?

In the beginning God created heavens and earth. The earth was empty and formless. Through Jesus all things were made, i.e., Earth, plants, animals, humankind.

The first three chapters of Genesis record that God made the cosmos and planet Earth. Can you imagine the pristine beauty of Earth at this time? God made everything with us in mind. Remember the words of a song that go something like: 'I want you to want me; I want you to love me.' God wants individuals on Earth to want and love him so much that God made the exquisite cosmos and Earth for them.

As this chapter showed, many cultures have overlapping creation stories. Water is common to most cultures' stories. Deities acted on primordial water to create dry land for plants, animals, and humans. Utopias are another common theme in ancient cultures. In most stories individual's accessed utopia after they died. Many early cultures have stories about trees, possibly because trees were tall, provided shelter, and lived long in comparison to the human life span.

A concern I have about trees in diverse cultures is that many are named "tree of life," i.e. in Chinese, Israelite, and Hindu cultures. Possibly, eating fruit from these trees doesn't give immortal life in the earthly realm. Instead eating tree-of-life fruit gives mortality when eaten in heaven (afterlife).

Common *Bible* themes, i.e. water, utopias, trees, among different cultures can be a problem for evangelists. Some think other cultures' legends are silly at best, abhorrent at worst. These evangelists accept only legends consistent with *Bible* lore. Still others chose to believe certain elements of a culture's stories of creation, utopias, and role of trees while rejecting other elements. Thus, they derive a personal, syncretistic model of creation. Their belief is a combination of views from many cultures.

So many creation stories have common elements. Cultural anthropologists suggested that creation stories across the globe have overlapping elements because at one time, all humankind had a common origin and culture. To many Christians, this perspective is appealing.

Commonalities in early cultures' beliefs can be used when telling others about the Christian view of creation, particularly when targets of evangelism ask for information or give their cultural perspective.

Because God created the entire earth and everything on it, his creation, to include humankind, owes him worship. A way we worship God is to believe in him and accept his free gift of salvation. A way we worship God is to tell others about him — to be an enthusiastic proponent of all he has done in creation and for us individually.

The *Bible* asks the question, how will individuals know about Jesus unless someone tells them (Romans 10:14). Telling is the evangelist's role. We don't need to tell targets everything we know about God and his Son. Start with sharing God's plan of salvation, Jesus as Redeemer. Evangelists don't need to start with discussions of creation of the world. Stick to the good news message of Jesus' redemptive work on the cross. At the same time, know what other cultures teach.

*****

In the *Bible* God created the world, then rested. God didn't need to rest; God never becomes tired. Most of the time, Christians think of rest as some form of relaxation. Bishop Robert Barron wrote that rest means "achievement of joy." God created the cosmos, planet Earth to include plants, animals, and humankind. Then, God metaphorically stepped back and felt joy at his achievement. Evangelists, also, can step back from their daily labors and feel joy in serving God. Remember, Jesus said that angels in heaven rejoice over one individuals who is saved (Luke 15:7). We are called to be perpetual (ongoing, continuous, never ceasing) evangelists. At the same time resting and feeling joy is okay. In fact, resting is so okay that God created a day for his people to rest and enjoy him.

Points to Ponder

1. Should every Christian be an evangelist? Who or why not?

2. Theologians proposed that many creation stories were similar because they were rooted in a common culture. In other words, all cultures have a single origin. What do you think?

3. How can evangelists use diverse cultural ideas about water, utopias, and trees in evangelism if these concepts are brought up by evangelism targets?

4. Go back through Chapter 2 noting all legends, beliefs, and traditions from Islamic culture and religion. Have any Muslim beliefs crept into the Christian faith? Which ones?

5. Cherokee natives with their belief that ancestors are in cedar trees, have pieces of cedar in their homes and around their necks. How does Christian's use of a cross or crucifix mirror how Cherokee use cedar wood?

6. Most individuals have a notion of hell. How are those notions similar to each other? How do they differ? Should the evangelist talk to targeted individuals about hell?

3

ADAM AND EVE

The first man was Adam and the first woman Eve (*Bible*). God created them. Adam lived over 900 years. If <u>legends</u> are accurate, Eve lived even longer. Many stories evolved around their life. None is more important than Adam and Eve's rebellion against their Creator. The next chapter (Chapter 4) drills down on that rebellion.

After the first couple rebelled against him, God expelled them from the Garden of Eden, their Paradise home. To prevent them from reentering Eden, God placed cherubim (a type of angel) at its entrance. The next page contains a scroll on cherubim; some of the information is from the *Bible*, some is legend.

<u>Latter-Day Saints (Mormons)</u> believe that Adam and Eve were the first parents, the first humans to live on the Earth. In the spirit world, Adam was named Michael, the archangel. He led the righteous against Satan. When Adam and Eve were first placed in the Garden of Eden, they weren't mortal. They couldn't have children and didn't die. They didn't yet chose between good and evil. Only after they chose rebellion against God, did they become mortal.

Cherubim

Judeo-Christian Tradition

A cherub is a spiritual celestial being. In the *Bible*, cherub (plural cherubim) are first mention when placed at the entrance of the Garden of Eden to prevent Adam and Eve from reentering.

Cherubim have contact with God. Their purpose is to serve God in the earthly realm.

Representations of two cherubim with wings were located on the Ark of the Covenant. These two representations are called the Cherubim of Glory.

Cherubim have four faces (ox, lion, eagle, and man) and four wings.

After Eden

In the *Qur'ān* (Islam) Adam was a great prophet. The Islamic religion accepts that Adam and Eve were the first humans. Eve was made from Adam. When Adam and Eve sinned they were expelled from their garden home. According to an Arabian legend, Adam took three plants from Eden:

- A stalk of wheat, the chief of all kinds of food.
- Dates from a date palm tree, the chief fruit.
- Myrtle, the chief of sweet-scented flowers.

Taking these three plants was smart. Adam could plant wheat (Einkorn wheat, *Triticum boeoticum)* kernels and have flour for bread, a staple in ancient people's diets. Dates were a high sugar fruit. The earliest date tree was the date palm tree (*Phoenix dactylifera*). The third plant that Adam took from the Garden of Eden was the myrtle (*Myrtus communis*), described as a sweet-scented flower. This legend resonates with us. Perhaps, even earliest humankind knew that in addition to food, they needed beauty, as found in the myrtle flower.

The Spanish Jewish scholar, Maimonides (16th century) mentioned a legend, cherished by the Nabateans (home around Petra, Jordan). Supposedly, Adam traveled to India and returned by way of Babylon. He carried a golden tree in blossom, a leaf that no fire could burn, two leaves each of which could cover an individual, and an enormous leaf plucked from a tree beneath whose branches 10,000 men could shelter. When I read this leaf legend, my reaction was that the leaf must have been difficult to transport.

Notice both preceding legends about Adam included plants. Plants were integral to lives of ancient humankind; yet many plant legends were just that — legends — not truth.

Cursed Land

After God expelled Adam and Eve from the Garden of Eden, the *Bible* recorded that they toiled (work, sweat) for food. God caused some plants to grow thorns and thistles. One scientific explanation for plant thorns and thistles is "plant adaption." Plants produced thorns and thistles to protect themselves from animals that eat them.

When I read about the scientific model of "plant adaptation" I questioned why all plants eaten by humans and animals didn't develop spines or thorns for protection. For millennia, wheat was grown and harvested. Wheat stalks show no sign of spine production.

A legend, possibly early Christian, is that the first thornbush that grew on earth was the Jerusalem thornbush (*Paliurus spina-christi*). Supposedly, the Jerusalem thornbush was used to make the crown of thorns placed on Jesus' head. Stems and twigs are flexible, ideal to braid into a crown. On the Jerusalem thornbush, thorns can be one inch long. They hurt soft head tissue. Despite the Jerusalem thorn's characteristics, there's no proof that the first thornbush was the Jerusalem thornbush. No evidence exists that Jesus' crown of thorns was made from the Jerusalem thornbush.

More about Eve

Most ancient cultures include stories about the first woman; sometimes the woman was a goddess. Many women had children. Often, children were gods, however, at times they were humans.

A <u>Mesopotamian</u> legend identified Adam's first wife, not as Eve, but Lilith. Like Adam, Lilith was formed from the dust of the earth, that is, from the soil. Lilith was created at the same time as Adam. Lilith believed she was equal to Adam. She wouldn't submit to Adam. As a result, Lilith left Adam and the Garden of Eden.

Another legend about Lilith was that Adam separated from Eve for a time. During that time, he sired demonic offspring with Lilith. In this legend, Lilith was pure evil, known to kill pregnant women and newborn infants. From ancient times through the Middle Ages, women wore amulets around their neck to ward off Lilith's evil. Often, Lilith was the subject of exorcism.

In the *Bible* the first woman's name was Eve. Her husband Adam gave her this name after the couple was expelled from the Garden of Eden (Genesis 3:20). The *Bible* recorded that God created Eve from Adam's rib. In an Israelite <u>Hebrew</u> legend, Adam named the woman created from his rib "*Hawwah,* " which in the Hebrew language means the "Mother of all things, or "first women." See a Mesopotamian legend similar to the story of Eve's creation on the next page.

Some Christian theologians contend that because Eve was created from Adam's rib, Eve was intended to be subservient to Adam. Present day study of body structure (anatomy) shows that both male and female genders have the same number of ribs. Males have an equal number of ribs on both sides of their body. No scientific evidence suggests that a rib was taken from the male body to create the female body.

Israelite/Jewish legends included stories about Eve. One legend claimed that when God created Adam and Eve, God divided Paradise. The east and north were assigned to Adam as were all male animals. Eve was mistress of the west and south and all female animals. In this legend, Adam and Eve had equal control in their world. This division of Paradise is restricted to Israelite/Jewish legend and not found in the *Bible*.

Murderous Children

Bible lore identified Cain and Abel as children of Adam and Eve; however, a more obscure legend said that Cain was conceived by God and Eve. In the *Bible*, Cain was Eve's first-born son and a farmer. Second-born son, Abel, kept flocks. Both occupations were valuable in ancient humankind's world. Cain murdered Abel. The murder was premeditated (Genesis 4:8). The *Bible* recorded that Cain was

Mother of Humankind

Mesopotamian Legend

The god Enki ate eight plants that belonged to the goddess Ninhursag. Ninhursag cursed Enki so that eight parts of Enki's body became diseased. When Enki was nearly dead, other gods persuaded Ninhursag to help him.

In response, Ninhursag created eight healing goddesses.

The goddess who cured Enki's rib was Ninti, whose name meant "lady of the rib" or "lady of life."

This Mesopotamian legend could have influenced the Genesis record of Eve's creation from Adam's rib angry that Abel's sacrifice was accepted by God, but his wasn't. See another motive for Cain's murder of Abel in the scroll on the next page.

One <u>university scholar</u> proposed that the conflict between Cain and Abel was an allegory describing the conflict between nomadic people (herders of flocks) and more settled farmers. The farmer, Cain, won over the more nomadic herder (Abel) by killing him.

Reentering Eden

A legend handed down by both <u>Israelites/Jews</u> and <u>Greeks</u> recounted that when Adam was around 900 years old, he overtaxed his strength when uprooting an enormous bush. Adam was in great pain; he thought he was dying. Adam sent his third son, Seth, to the Garden of Eden. Adam told Seth to bring him ambrosia (the oil of mercy) from the tree of life so Adam could be healed.

At the entrance to the Garden of Eden, cherubim allowed Seth to enter. When Seth approached the tree of life, Seth saw a youth, radiant as the sun, sitting on the tree of life. The youth told Seth that he was the Son of God who would one day come to earth to deliver humankind from sin. Not until that time would God give the oil of mercy to Adam or his offspring.

An <u>Israelite/Jewish</u> teaching claimed that the angel that guarded the tree of life handed Seth three small seeds. The angel told Seth to place the seeds in Adam's mouth when Adam was buried. Seth obeyed the angel. Each seed took root. The seeds became the

Motive for Murder

Israelite Legend

A legend is that Cain wasn't the son of Adam. Instead, Cain was the son of Eve and Satan when Satan took the form of the angel Samael. Samael was so beautiful that Eve couldn't resist him. From birth, Cain was the son of evil.

The *Bible* recorded that Cain killed Abel because Cain was jealous that God accepted Abel's offering, but didn't accept Cain's offering.

Legend offered another reason for Cain's animosity toward Abel. Cain and Abel were destined to marry their sisters. Both men wanted to marry the same sister.

The sister preferred Abel. In a jealous rage, Cain murdered Abel Whether or not the sister married Cain wasn't recorded.

olive (*Olea europaea*), cedar (*Cedrus libani*), and cypress (*Cupressus sempervirens*) trees, all three valuable trees in the ancient near East environment.

The cedar tree's centrality among ancient peoples is seen in legends of other cultures. In the *Epic of Gilgamesh*, an ancient <u>Sumerian</u> legend, the home of the gods was named Cedar Mountain. A legend about the cedar tree in the <u>Cherokee</u> nation (Ancestors) is in Chapter 2, Creation, Paradise.

Another <u>Israelite/Jewish</u> legend averred that when Adam and Eve's son, Seth, entered the Garden of Eden, Eve went with Seth. There, Eve received one-half of an uneaten apple from an angel. The angel directed Eve to plant apple seeds where Adam died. In this legend, Eve outlived Adam. The apple half could have been the origin of the legend that the tree of knowledge of good and evil was an apple tree.

Adam's Death

Adam lived about 930 years (Genesis 5:5). Most legends agree that his son, Seth, was responsible for both Adam and Eve's burials. The *Bible* gave no information on where Adam was buried.

<u>Israelite/Jewish</u> tradition places Adam and Eve's burial site in the cave of Machpelah, a cave in a wooded field near Hebron, Israel. You read more about this cave in Section B of this book. A legend recorded that Adam chose to be buried in the cave at Machpelah because it was an entrance to the Garden of Eden. Adam came back to his roots, where God placed him at his creation.

A Christian tradition places the tomb of Adam in Jerusalem. A legend averred that Adam's burial site and Jesus' crucifixion site were the same place.

An Islamic legend is that Adam's body was taken into the ark at the time of the flood. After the flood, Adam's body was buried in the Cave of the Treasure (which refers to the Machpelah cave). Muslim exegetes suggested that Adam was buried at Muslim holy sites. Adam's head is buried at Hebron and his legs in the Dome of the Rock in Jerusalem.

Likely, Adam was buried between the Tigris and Euphrates Rivers, the historic location of the Garden in Eden. Initially, Adam's grave may have been marked. A few hundred years after Adam's death, a great flood occurred in that part of the world. Adam's grave site was destroyed and Adam's remains dispersed by the flood.

Eve's Death

Israelite legend contended that Eve outlived Adam. Between Adam's death and her death, Eve spent her time weeping. Eve's distress was caused by not knowing what became of Adam's body. In this legend, an angel interred Adam's body when Eve was asleep. When the hour of Eve's death approached, Eve prayed that God would allow her to be buried with Adam. I could find no legend that God answered Eve's prayer.

What about Evangelism?

God created humankind, both male and female, in his own image.

The *Bible* gives proportionally little information about the first man and woman created by God. In the years following creation, humankind created many legends about these seminal characters. You have read a few in this chapter. Some may be true, many are lies.

I marveled at the dichotomous accounts of Eve in Israelite/Jewish literature. In one legend, Eve is equal with Adam. In another, she leads Adam into rebellion against God. Importantly, evangelists talk to both males and females. In the 21st century identifying that a female (Eve) was responsible for sin entering the world will immediately alienate women and some men.

Many 21st individuals, even Christians, don't believe that Adam and Eve were real persons. Rather, they were archetypes of individuals who progressed from living in harmony with God to rebelling against him. Adam and Eve were placed in the *Bible* to make a point, i.e., humankind sins and needs a Savior.

Almost all evangelists encounter questions about God creating the first couple versus scientific theories of life on Earth and evolution. Don't go down that rabbit trail! Often, questions about creation are a ploy to move the evangelist away from the salvation message. Individuals can hold diverse opinions on how creation occurred and still be redeemed by belief in Jesus.

Remember(!), the truth that an evangelist must tell nonbelievers doesn't focus on God's creation of the first couple. An evangelist is called to tell others (targets, individuals) about the indisputable Jesus Christ and his redeeming work on the cross, followed by his resurrection. The story of Adam and Eve is an arresting *Bible* story but knowing, even believing, the story isn't required for salvation.

If an evangelists has to answer a targeted individual about beliefs encounter in the *Bible* story of Adam and Eve, here are several options:

- First, the evangelist can adhere to the *Bible* story that Adam and Eve were actual humans created by God.
- Second, an evangelist can accept current scientific evidence that humankind has been present on Earth for hundreds of thousands of years. This particular belief isn't denied by the first three chapters of Genesis. God said that in his eyes a thousand years are like a day or a watch in the night. (Psalm 90:4). On a city wall the watchman's shift could be as short as 2-3 hours.
- Third, an evangelist can use the concept of intelligent design, that is, God created humankind but did so over many millennia. This notion has two advantages. It is consistent with fossil remains of humankind on Earth. Intelligent design

emphasizes that humankind's timeline differs from God's timeline.

- Fourth, rarely considered nor discussed is that time in the Garden of Eden moved at a different pace than on the remainder of Earth. Eons outside the Garden of Eden may have equaled one day (24-hour period) inside the Garden.

In the Bible, God created Adam and Eve, the first humans, and placed them on Earth. Adam and Eve didn't have any choice in their creation. It was God choice. Jesus, the Son of God, had a choice to come to earth as a neonate with Mary as mother and the Holy Spirit as father. Jesus could have said "No, not interested, not going to do that. I know all things and I know the end of the story—I'm going to be abused and killed."

Jesus didn't do that. Jesus said "Yes" to his father. Jesus came to Earth so that evangelist would have a message of forgiveness to share with friends and nonfriends.

Points to Ponder

1. Is Genesis history, science, or literature?

2. Should the story of Adam and Eve be used in your evangelism? How will you respond when you are asked about these two *Bible* characters?

3. Develop your own legend about something that happened around one event in Chapter 3, Adam and Eve.

4. Would an external reviewer say that *Bible* lore influenced your legend or that your legend influenced *Bible* lore?

5. Reread the four possible responses to an individual who tells you they don't believe the Adam and Eve story. Which response, if any, are you most likely to use in your personal evangelism?

6. Go back through Chapter 3 noting all legends, beliefs, traditions from Mormon culture and religion. Have any Mormon beliefs entered into your church's doctrine and faith. Which ones?

4

SIN IN CREATION

For early Egyptians, the ideal way of life was harmony and order called Ma'at. The opposite of Ma'at was disharmony and trouble, named Isfet Ma'at. Ma'at couldn't exist without Isfet Ma'at and vice versa; they were dualistic.

A popular tale from the Egyptian Middle Kingdom (2050-1650 BCE), the "*Moaning of the Bedouin*," summarizes the Egyptian perspective on sin:

Those who destroy the lie promote Ma'at,
Those who promote the good will erase the evil.
As fulness casts out appetite,
as clothes cover the nude and
as heaven clears up after a storm.

The Egyptian perspective on sin caused me to think of God-Satan, good-evil. Could one occur without the other? Would humankind fully understand what is good without understanding what is evil?

The focus of the Yoruba (Nigeria, Africa) religion is on living a "good" life. For Yorubans there is no need for salvation by grace. Yorubans believe in reincarnation, but they don't try to escape successive rebirths. Rather, rebirth is a reward. Defiant individuals, i.e., ones who commit suicide and cruel individuals, aren't reborn.

In Judeo-Christian perspectives, knowledge of sin assumes knowing right from and wrong. See the scroll on the next page for Judeo-Christian perspectives on sin.

Muslim's view sin as going against commands of Allah (God), or breaches of laws in the *Qur'ān*, the Islamic holy book. In it, sin is an act and not a state of being. Muslims don't think of themselves as sinners. For instance, if I believe the Muslim faith, I'm not a sinner, but I sin.

On Judgment Day Allah weighs individuals' good deeds against their bad deeds. Allah punishes individuals whose evil deeds outweigh good deeds. Muslims believe God forgave Adam his disobedience. Adam's disobedient act isn't viewed as "original" sin in the *Qur'ān*.

Mormons believe that the Heavenly Father gave Adam and Eve agency. Agency is the freedom to choose whether or not they would obey God's command to not eat from the tree of knowledge of good and evil. If they obeyed God, they could remain in the Garden of Eden; however, they wouldn't grow, progress, or learn by challenges in lives. Adam and Eve's choice to disobey God was part of God's plan.

According to Mormons, sin is wilful disobedience of God's laws. Humans can be restored to God by admitting their rebellion, repenting of it, and asking God for restoration. Mormons believe that Adam and Eve asked God for forgiveness and were forgiven. For Mormons the restored individual must abandon sinful acts and live a righteous life going forward.

Perspectives on Sin

Judeo-Christian Tradition

Rebellion, revolt, defiance against God's laws.

Failure to measure up to standards laid down by God.

Highly reprehensible acts.

Culturally prohibited acts.

Passivity in the face of injustice.

In order to sin, there must be a prohibition against the conduct.

God forgives and punishes sin.

Satan entices individuals to sin.

In the *Bible* sin entered the world because humankind disobeyed God. God forbid humankind from eating fruit from the tree of knowledge of good and evil. Like most of us who are told not to do something, the prohibited attracts us. The tree and its fruit attracted the first humans.

An Israelite/Jewish legend described a snake as the emissary of Satan who tempted Eve to eat forbidden fruit. This same legend claimed that a fig was the original fruit eaten by Eve. When Eve ate the fig, all other trees in the Garden of Eden lost their leaves. Fig leaves were the only ones that remained for Adam and Eve to use for clothes.

In contrast to the *Bible's* view that Adam was with Eve when the snake tempted her, Israelite/Jewish legend presents a different picture. According to Jewish legend, Eve went to Adam and prevailed upon him to eat the forbidden fruit. By placing Adam in a separate location from Eve when she was deceived by the serpent, Eve intentionally led Adam into rebellion against God.

The *Bible* recorded that after Adam and Eve's rebellion against God, they knew the difference between right and wrong. They understood sin. Further, Adam and Eve were ashamed of their nakedness. Adam and Eve had few options for body coverings. Animals didn't die; neither were animals killed for their hides.

Adam and Eve created clothing from fig tree (*Ficus carica*) leaves (Genesis 3:7). The fig tree had large leaves. Few fig leaves were needed to create body coverings. Later, God killed animals — the same animals that he created and breathed into the breath of life — to make clothes for Adam and Eve. Animal skins covered the shame of their naked bodies.

Modern scientists, particularly archeologists, aver that the first humankind used animal skins for clothing, not plant leaves. Early humankind's cave paintings showed animal skins as clothes. Little evidence exists that early humans covered themselves with plant-based clothing; however, plant-based clothing would have deteriorated over millennia and not remained as prototypes for 21st century scientists to find.

My Wrong Belief

I was born and reared in central Pennsylvania in an area settled by Germans and Scot Irish. I grew up believing that the tree of knowledge of good and evil was an apple tree and its fruit an apple. My family had a huge apple tree in the yard. We never ate apples from the tree. No apple pies!

The legend that the apple tree was the original tree of knowledge of good and evil could be related to its Latin name, *Malus domestica*. In Latin, the word *mălum* is translated as evil, calamity, or harm. Possibly, the closeness of the Latin words *mălum* and *Malus* accounted for individuals identifying the tree of knowledge of good and evil as an apple tree.

Several days ago, I watched a video on sin entering the world produced by a Christian church. A picture of an apple was shown as the vehicle for entry of sin. The legend that the original fruit that Adam and Eve ate was an apple has become so much a part of Christian culture that it is rarely questioned.

Despite the <u>legend</u> that the tree of knowledge of good and evil was an apple tree, likely that legend is a lie. The proposed location of the Garden of Eden is between the Tigris and Euphrates Rivers in Iraq. <u>Scientists</u> reported that in this area soil is sandy, climate dry. Annual rainfall is about 13 inches.

<u>Botanical studies</u> document that apple trees thrive best in temperate climates where there is deep, well-drained loam soil. Ideally, apple trees receive 39-49 inches of rainfall annually, distributed over the apple-growing season. If apple trees grew between the Tigris and Euphrates Rivers, likely trees didn't produce a fine variety of apple that would entice Adam and Eve to disobey God.

What about Evangelism?

In Judeo-Christianity, the first humankind (Adam and Eve) sinned by rebelling against God, that is doing something God told them not to do.
Through Adam and Eve sin entered the world.

Words of a late 20th century song were something like: "It took time for me to know, what you tried so hard not to show." Adam and Eve tried to hide their rebellion from God using fig leaves and avoiding God's presence. Individuals, an evangelist interacts with, often try to hide their pain and failures. They project that they have it all together. Rarely, if ever, is that true.

How do you react to receiving a robocall or a solicitation call from someone you don't know. Pretty negatively even if you are a patient person and a temperate Christian. That's how an individual will respond if an evangelist accosts them on the street, office, etc., and starts to talk about Jesus to them. That evangelist has no relationship or credibility with targeted individuals. They will ignore the evangelist. Possibly, the approach turns them off to future discussions about Jesus as Redeemer.

Importantly, the evangelist isn't a psychologist. He/she shouldn't attempt to analyze a target's behaviors. That's another rabbit trail that the evangelist should avoid. An evangelist's purpose is to share the saving knowledge of Jesus Christ.

Adam and Eve's rebellion (sin, disobedience) occurred many millennia ago; yet sin remains an important and uncomfortable phenomenon among Judeo-Christians in the 21st century. Not every culture (i.e., Yoruba, Muslims) has a severe perspective on sin. Some cultures don't postulate the need for a Redeemer, a perfect man-god to die for sins of humans.

Recently, an Episcopal priest told the following story: A man came to him and asked to be baptized. The priest asked why the man wanted to be baptized, considering the man never attended church. The reply was, "So I go to heaven when I die." Evangelists encounter many men (women, children) like this man who confused redemption and baptism. Some Christian churches even teach that baptism alone without redemption is the pass key to heaven.

Christian church theologians and pastors talk and write about the doctrine of original sin. In this doctrine, present-day humans are born with a tainted nature. I think of this inherited tainted nature as similar to a genetic-inherited disease. In this view, humans tend to sin just as an individual who inherits the diabetes mellitus gene tends to develop diabetes mellitus. Some Christian faith perspectives assert that each human must be baptized to rid themselves of original sin—the sin of Adam. This perspective baptizes infants.

Other Christian faith perspectives baptizes individuals when they understand right from wrong. Individuals who hold this perspective believe that each individual can make a conscious decision to follow, or not follow, Jesus.

Religions such as Islam don't include baptism as a religious rite. Recently, I learned that an African church doesn't have a baptismal service. Baptism is replaced by a handshake. Mormons baptize when an individual is accountable. Mormons have the option for being baptized for dead ancestors who weren't baptized into the faith.

I am positive that evangelists don't need to get into discussions about when to baptize, even how to baptize, i.e., full immersion, sprinkling. What is important is admitting we are sinners and accepting Jesus as Savior to rid ourselves of sin. Jesus Christ, the son of God, died and rose for sins. Redemption through faith in Jesus the Christ is different from baptism.

Today, is Good Friday in my Christian faith. It is a celebration of the day that Jesus was crucified, not for his sins, but for mine. The perfect, sinless Son of God died for me. In two days, it will be Easter (Resurrection Day). Jesus' tomb will be empty. Jesus rose from the dead. As evangelists we should concentrate on Jesus' act of redemption when we tell others about Christian salvation. We can also concentrate on Jesus resurrection which points toward the truth that Jesus-believers will be resurrected.

Points to Ponder

1. Write out your definition of sin. What are your favorite sins? The ones you commit over and over again — the ones you don't plan to stop committing?

2. Is sin an archaic (old fashioned) perspective and shouldn't be discussed in 21st century evangelism?

3. Some cultures have no definition of sin for which they need a Redeemer? How could these cultures be correct? How could they be incorrect? Why should the evangelist know about them?

4. Was it necessary for humankind to sin (rebel against God) in order to develop knowledge of right and wrong? If we don't know what is wrong, can we know what is right?

5. How did Adam and Eve having naked bodies correspond to having their minds/thoughts on display? How do we attempt to cover our thoughts?

6. Go back throughout the chapter noting all legends, beliefs, traditions. I don't know where many came from. Have any of these beliefs crept into the Christian faith?

5

A FLOOD

In the *Bible* narrative, God used water to destroy creation. Water was an environmental weapon. Not infrequently, evangelists are asked, "Why would a loving God weld such a weapon?" The answer is that God became so grieved by humankind's sin that he regretted making and placing humankind on earth (Genesis 6:5-8). God wanted to cleanse planet Earth.

Much happened in the millennia after God created humankind and Adam and Eve were expelled from the Garden of Eden. Cain murdered Abel. Cain was exiled from his home. Cain's offspring crafted musical instruments, forged tools out of bronze and iron, and built cities. Humankind lost all morality, i.e., they practiced polygamy (Genesis 6:1-4). Possibly, females mated with fallen angels. From these Genesis descriptions, do you get the sense that humankind forgot God? Seem familiar?

Noah

Noah was righteous and blameless among the people of his time (Genesis 6:9). God instructed Noah to build a waterproof ark, put rooms in it, and three decks (Genesis 6:11-7:4). God planned to wipe the Earth of creatures with the breath of life in them.

Noah, his wife, three sons and their wives, along with pairs of all living animals entered the ark when it was completed; thus, the earth could repopulate. *Bible* age calculations estimate that Noah was born about 136 years after Adam's death. In this timeline, the time between Adam's creation and Noah's birth is calculated as 1065 years. Likely, this calculation is incorrect. The time could have been much longer.

An Israelite/Jewish legend proposes that Noah didn't marry until he was in the fourth century of life. Noah sired three sons: Shem, Ham, and Japheth. God limited Noah to three sons to ensure there was adequate space in the ark for sons and their wives.

Islamic teachings have stories about Noah who is named Nuh in the *Qur'ān*. Nuh was a great prophet who warned the people to turn from sin and worship Allah. Nuh's prophecy and preaching spanned over 900 years. The people refused Nuh's message, even mocked him.

Allah instructed Nuh to build an ark to save himself and family. When the ark was completed, Nuh loaded it with his household, pairs of every animal, and food. Islamic tradition teaches that Nuh had four sons. One son didn't believe in Allah and refused to enter the ark. That son believed that he could flee to the mountains and escape the flood.

Flood Epics

In addition to Israelites, other ancient civilizations had flood legends. In the list below all are Mesopotamian exception the Yoruba:

- Sumerian: *Epic of Ziusudra*
- Akkadian: *Atrahasis Epic*
- Babylonian: *Epic of Gilgamesh*
- Yoruba: *Flood of Ife*

The Gilgamesh epic (dated before 2000 BCE) is the most complete flood account. It was the most widespread poem of antiquity. The *Epic of Gilgamesh* recorded that pre-flood Noah's hometown was Shruppak on the banks of the Euphrates River. There, Noah was a wealthy leader.

Overlap occurs in the *Bible* account of Noah's flood and the flood story in the Gilgamesh epic. See Table 5.1 for a comparison of information found in the *Epic of Gilgamesh* and the *Bible* account. Overlap between the two accounts is in topics rather than specific content of topics. For example, both accounts has a deity announcing the flood to a man, all use birds to assess earth's dryness, and all recorded a length that the rain fell on the earth. Scholars believe the Gilgamesh epic preceded the *Bible* story of Noah and the flood.

Most of us remember seeing pictures of the ark from *Bible* storybooks. In those books, the front (bow or prow) of the ark was always pointed and often the

Table 5.1 Comparison of *Bible* and Gilgamesh Flood Accounts.

Topic	Noah's Flood	Gilgamesh Epic
Why the flood occurred?	Degenerate behavior of humankind	Gods couldn't sleep because of human's noise
Who built boat?	God told Noah to build an ark	Ea (god) warned Utnapishtim to convert his house to a boat
How long to build boat?	Up to 120 years	7 days
Characteristics of boat?	Rectangle, 3 stories	Cube-shaped, 7 stories
Humans saved?	Noah, wife, 3 sons & wives	Utnapishtim & kin
How long rain lasted?	40 days & nights	After 7th day, grew calm
Where boat landed?	Ararat (Turkey) mountains	Mount Nisir (Iraq, Kurdistan)
Extent of flood?	Entire Earth & mountains	No specifics on extent or depth
Animals in boat?	Male & female animals, birds, reptiles	All wild & tame creatures
Birds sent out to see if earth dry?	Raven first, then a dove	Dove, swallow, then raven.

back (stern) was narrowed. In actuality, the ark was rectangular (Genesis 6:14-17). The ark had no need of a bow or stern because the ark didn't move forward through the water; nor was it steered by a rudder on the back. Instead, the ark was designed to float on the top of the water and to withstand the impact of rain and flood waters. Depicts of the ark with a pointed front and back is legend.

Several years ago, we visited the Ark Encounter in Kentucky, United States. A supposed replica of Noah's ark was constructed there. Unlike Noah's ark, the Kentucky ark has a pointed bow and a narrowed stern with a rudder.

Only Noah and those with him in the ark survived the flood (*Bible*). They (8 individuals) remained in the ark over a year. When waters receded from the earth, the ark rested on a peak in the Ararat mountains in eastern Turkey.

Extent of the Flood

One of the most controversial aspect of _Bible_ lore is whether or not there was a global flood or a flood localized to the ancient near East. The *Bible* asserts that the flood was global.

Most scientists concluded that there was no global flood. Nevertheless, almost all cultures have a flood legend, to include Australian aborigines, Chinese, Japanese, Norse, Egyptian, Sumerian, Babylonian, Greek, Aztec, Nigerian, etc. The Flood of Ile is a legend from the Yoruba people of Nigeria, Africa

See the scroll in the next page for a flood account from western Africa. In it, the flood didn't cover the entire Earth.

Christians can't help contemplating whether or not the flood actually happened. Most conclude: Yes, a flood occurred.   Then, a question about the extent of the flood rises. Was the flood limited to only the ancient near East or was it worldwide?

Scientists who specialize in the study of soil and rock sediment/strata concluded that there are large areas of the Earth that showed no evidence of a global flood. Further, in millennia prior to the projected date of Noah's flood, studies of rock and sediment showed evidence of earlier massive floods in the
Mesopotamian region.

Women of the Ark

Four women lived in the ark. Likely, they supplied it with food prior to the flood. Five times in Genesis, the *Bible* recorded "Noah's wife." Not once was her name given. The only information given on Noah's wife was that she was Noah's kinswoman. Although the *Bible* recorded the names of Noah's sons—Ham, Shem, and Japheth—their wives' names weren't recorded.

The women in the ark were named in other publications. Their names varied with the publication. The *Book of Jubilees*, a noncanonical ancient text written before the birth of Jesus, gave their names as:

The Flood of Ife*

Yoruba (African Legend)

Obatala, the sky god and creator, founded Ife, the first Yoruban town. Ife prospered, becoming a city. Gods were happy with what Obatala did except for Olokun, the ruler of all below the sky.

Olokun was angry that Obatala usurped much of her kingdom. Olokun summoned great waves of vast oceans and sent them surging across the land.

Much of the land was underwater, many people drowned. People who survived beseeched Eshu, the messenger god, to report what was happening in Ife.

When the chief god, Orunmila, heard the news, he cast spells causing the flood waters to retreat. Dry land reappeared, and so ended the great flood.

- Noah's wife: Emzara (Naamah)
- Ham's wife: Na'eltama'uk
- Shem's wife: Sedeqetelabab
- Japheth's wife: 'Adataneses

A <u>Jewish</u> story focused on Noah's wife. In this story she was named Naamah. Just as God told Noah to take a male and female of each animal into the ark, God directed Naamah to gather two seeds of each flower, trees, and other plants. When Naamah left the ark, she felt the soft moist earth under her feet. Naamah planted each of the seeds in the earth. God told Naamah that he would make her guardian of all living plants. For a single moment, Naamah saw into the future when plants covered the entire earth.

In one <u>Islamic</u> legend, Naamah wasn't a believer in Allah. She didn't join Nuh on the ark. An <u>Arab</u> legend described an episode about Ham's wife. God instructed Noah to destroy the first person who announced the flood's beginning. Ham's wife was baking bread in an oven. When water rushed from the oven, she exclaimed that the flood was starting. Supposedly, God cancelled his command that the first person who announced the flood should be killed so that Noah didn't have to kill his son's wife.

Safe to Disembark

After rain ceased and waters began to recede, Noah sent birds from the ark to learn if dry places were present on earth (Genesis 8:11, *Bible*). Eventually, a dove returned to Noah with a freshly plucked olive leaf (*Olea europaea*). Noah concluded that some

Earth's surfaces were dry. Soon afterward, Noah left the ark.

This story is the first time that the olive tree is named in the *Bible*. Possibly, the olive tree and its products weren't present on earth before the flood, however, that possibility is unlikely. More plausibly, Noah took olives, olive oil, and even olive tree saplings into the ark.

By Israelite/Jewish legend, after leaving the ark, each of Noah's sons built a city and named it after his wife. Neither the *Bible* nor legend record that Noah fathered additional offspring.

Signs of Peace

To ancient Israelites, the olive tree, branch, and leaf were associated with peace. Having the dove bring an olive leaf to Noah in the ark was a sign of God's peace toward humankind.

The first rainbow appeared on Earth after the flood. The rainbow was God's promise that he would never again destroy the Earth by water (Genesis 9:12-16). A rainbow is a multi-colored arc in the sky caused by reflecting, bending, and dispersing light in water droplets in the sky. Usually, rainbows appear in a section of sky directly opposite the sun. Because the rainbow's appearance can be explained scientifically, doesn't negate it as a sign of God's covenant with humankind.

An Irish legend associated with the rainbow is that a pot of gold, protected by a leprechaun, is found at the end of the rainbow. If viewed from an airplane, the rainbow is a circle, not an arc; consequently, the end of the rainbow can never be pinpointed.

Noah's Death

Noah lived approximately 350 years after the flood and died when he was approximately 950 years old (Genesis 9:28-29). One Israelite/Jewish legend claimed Noah remained in eastern Turkey for about 100 years after he left the ark. Then, Noah decided that the area was too populated. He traveled to Africa, then to Spain, and later settled in Italy. According to legend, Noah was the first ruler of Italy.

Possibly, Noah was alive when Abraham was born. Many *Bible* scholars speculated on whether or not the two men met. The ancient *Book of Jasher* averred that Abraham lived with Noah about 40 years. During those years, Noah taught Abraham about God. No biblical records tells of a meeting between Noah and Abraham. Further, if other ancient legends are correct, Noah was in Italy while Abraham was in Ur or Paddan Aram (Mesopotamia) during the later years of Noah's life.

What about Evangelism?

After the flood, God showed Noah a rainbow. God said that the rainbow was the sign of a covenant between God and humankind. The covenant was for God to never again destroy all life.

When you read the biblical account of Noah's flood, what message for your life did you take away from the episode? As an evangelist what did you learn of use to convince targeted individuals that they need a Savior.

As I was musing about flood questions aloud to my friend over lunch, she asked, "Does it matter whether the flood was global or local?" What do you think? Does a localized flood versus a global flood make a difference in your faith in God?

More importantly, does it make a difference in what you include in your evangelism message? If a global flood didn't occurred — for example a flood in Australia or South America — does it take away from the message that humankind must pay a price for sin against God? Does it take away from the message of Jesus' redemption? I think not, however, some Christians believe differently.

The evangelist takeaway from the biblical account of a flood is more important than the extent of a flood. That take away is that just as God punished sin in the days of Noah, God will punish sin in the 21st century. True, God is kind and loving, long in patience; yet, as the book of Revelations recorded a time will come when God punishes individuals who don't accept his Son as their Savior just as God punished people on Earth in the time of Noah.

Not one of us wants to be the reason someone doesn't spend eternity with God. No one wants the guilt of seeing someone in Hell because of something they didn't do, namely telling others about the work of Jesus. True, not all individuals an evangelist tells, or tries to tell, about Jesus want to hear or act on the message, nonetheless, evangelists are God's messengers on Earth. Their responsibility is to spread the message of salvation.

Evangelist shouldn't threaten targets of their message. Individuals shouldn't be led to a saving knowledge of Jesus through coercion, fear, or bullying. At the same time, evangelists have the responsibility to tell targets the end of the story of life on Earth. Also, evangelists need to alter their style of presenting the message to targeted individuals.

As I was preparing to write this section, I watched several computer videos on evangelism. One presented the evangelist telling the message of salvation to two individuals. One was a young Asian woman who appeared mild mannered, even timid. The second was an adult male who was confident. The evangelist didn't alter his tone or presentation style. He used the same style, mannerisms, voice volume and tone for both individuals. The evangelist's style was appropriate for the adult male but was intimidating for the young woman.

The end of the Bible story is that Jesus will come again in power as judge over all individuals. Those who accept Jesus as Savior will enter into eternal bliss with Jesus. Those individuals who haven't accepted Jesus as Savior enter into never-ending torment.

Points to Ponder

1. Put yourself in the position of an individual living in Noah's day. You see a man (actually, a highly credible man) building a huge water-proof boat. What would you think about him? What would you ask him? Remember, it never rained before the flood, i.e., water came up from the soil and watered the earth.

2. Will you use the story of Noah's flood in your evangelism? If so, how will you insert it?

3. As an evangelist what are you going to tell the targets of your evangelism about consequences of not accepting Jesus as Redeemer?

4 Why did women before, during, and after the ark episode get little attention in the *Bible*? Why did the ark women receive more attention in other books, i.e., the *Book of Jubilees*, *Book of Jasher,* than in the *Bible*?

5. Do you think that scientific theory that a global flood didn't occur is accurate? Scientists base their reasoning on soil/sediment across the globe.

6. Go back throughout the chapter noting all scientific theories and beliefs. Have any of these beliefs crept into the Christian faith?

6

DE-VOLUTION

After disembarking from the ark, Noah planted a vineyard (Genesis 9:20). *Bible* readers ask where did Noah get the grape vines (*Vitis vinifera*)? An answer is that Noah took vines into the ark. After leaving the ark, Noah planted these vines.

An alternative explanation is that Noah found grapevines in the post-flood world. Noah transplanted grapevines, growing at variable distances from his home, into land near his home. This second scenario assumes that grapevines stayed submerged in water for a minimum of one year after the flood.

Despite seeing God's devastating punishment for sin, after the flood the righteous Noah's behavior degenerated. Noah made wine from grapes, drank the wine, and became drunk. Noah passed out and lay drunk in his tent.

Ham made fun of Noah's naked body while Noah was drunk (Genesis 9:20-23). Further, Jewish sages postulated that while Noah was drunk, Ham entered Noah's tent and had sex with Noah's wife. The offspring of Ham and Noah's wife was Canaan. This incest story has little verification in biblical text, but may explain why Noah cursed Canaan rather than Ham.

Non-Humans on Earth

Islam teaches that Adam and descendants weren't the first beings on earth. They replaced another species called jinn. In Islam, jinn are invisible to the human eye. Jinn were created from smokeless fire. Most jinn were diabolical so Allah destroyed them and created humankind. The *Qur'ān* recorded at present time jinn can be good or evil. Some have converted to Islam and follow the prophet Mohammed.

Mormons believe that individuals preexisted before coming to and living on Earth in human bodies. They preexisted as spirits with God. Once they were born as earthly beings, these spirits didn't remember their pre-existent lives.

Many cultures believed that giants once lived on earth. In the *Bible* they were named Nephilim. The *Bible* suggested that Nephilim lived concurrently with Adam and Eve and after Adam and Eve. See the scroll on the next page that gives legends about Nephilim origins.

Nephilim translates from a Hebrew word as "fallen ones." Only a scant number of *Bible* verses referred to Nephilim (Genesis 6:1-4; Numbers 13:33; Job 1:6; Ezekiel 32:27). Nephilim appeared in various Israelite/Jewish sacred writings, not only the *Bible*. Recently, I watched a video that "documented" that clans of giants once lived in ancient United States.

Origins of Nephilim

Judeo-Christian Traditions

Four perspectives evolved on origins of Nephilim:

#1: Fallen angels copulated with daughters of men. Most popular view in Christian church.

#2: Demons possessed men and had offspring. The result was Nephilim.

#3: "Sons of God" means Seth's offspring. Most popular view among scholars.

#4: Sons of God were fallen men. Nephilim were offspring of fallen men (not angels) who married ungodly women.

The sexual interactions between fallen angels and daughters of men were believed to be a reason God caused Noah's flood. Despite this possible flood cause, Nephilim-type giants were documented in the *Bible* after Noah's flood. For example, Nephilim were present around Hebron when Israelites spied out Canaan and entered Canaan (Numbers 13:30-33). The giant Philistine warrior, Goliath, was thought to be a Nephilim.

In Arab legend the people of Ad (*Qur'ān* 26:130) were giants. They weren't destroyed in the flood because they were too tall, i.e., up to 100 feet. God destroyed the people of Ad later because they rejected his warnings. After their death Adites were banished into the lower layers of Hell.

Nimrod

Nimrod was an ancient mighty man and king who lived in the Mesopotamia area after the flood of Noah's time. Nimrod was the great grandson of Noah through Noah's son Ham (Genesis 10:8-12).

A legend (Israelite/Jewish) taught that Noah's son, Ham, had the animal hide clothes that God made for Adam. Ham gave the clothes to Nimrod who wore them when he went to war. The clothes kept Nimrod from being killed by his enemies.

As you read through the next chapters, you will notice that the name Nimrod appears in Abraham and Esau's lives. In one story Nimrod attempts to kill Abraham. In another Esau kills Nimrod.

Building a Tower

In early centuries after the flood of Noah's time, humankind lived between the Tigris and Euphrates Rivers. Most lived on the plain of Shinar (Genesis 11:1-4). They spoke a common language.

According to Israelite/Jewish legend, King Nimrod determined to build a tower — the Tower of Babel — that reached heaven. King Nimrod's reasons included:

- Humans could retreat to the Tower if another flood occurred.
- Humans would reach heaven, wage war against God, and kill everyone in Heaven.
- Nimrod would set up and worship his gods at the top of the Tower.
- Nimrod would place his throne at the top of the Tower and be worshiped there.

Workers made the tower from sunbaked bricks. Supposedly, 6000 men worked on the tower. The tower was shaped as a ziggurat (step appearance) rather than the Egyptian-style pyramid with smooth sides. Women were involved in brickmaking. Tower builders were so intent on building that when a woman gave birth she tied the neonate's body around her body and continued brick making.

God's Reaction

God was distressed by reasons humankind was building the Tower of Babel (Genesis 11:1-9). As a result, God confused or confounded the language of builders. They could no longer understand each other's words. Building couldn't progress without reliable communication. The result of God confounding humankind's language was that individuals with a common language banded together. Groups left the Shinar plain. They dispersed throughout the world.

Notice, God didn't destroy the earth again. Perhaps, God thought it was futile to keep destroying his creation. Humankind was going to continue to sin.

What about Evangelism?

*Come let us go down and confuse their language ......
so the Lord scattered them from there (Shinar) all
over the earth.*

Several generations after Noah's flood, God confounded the language of humankind. In the United States many individuals don't speak English. An evangelist who speaks only English won't be effective telling non-English speakers about Jesus.

When I lived in El Paso, Texas, 80% of the population was Latino. Spanish/Mexican was the primary language of grade and middle schools and in the *barrios* (ward, quarter, district) where Latino migrants lived. There, most adults weren't fluent in English. Local stores, i.e., Home Depot, hired only bilingual (English/Mexican) individuals as clerks.

In most of the El Paso community, an evangelist had to speak Spanish/Mexican fluently. Further, the evangelist was more effective if both Latino and male. The Latino culture remains male dominant.

Among White, English-speaking individuals in the United States, women and men are approaching equality. That isn't true in many other countries and many non-White subcultures in the United States. Evangelists must be aware of language and cultural differences if they want to be effective.

Often, evangelists believe because they speak a language, i.e., Spanish, they will be effective when telling immigrants about Jesus as Redeemer. Rarely, is that the case. Language nuances among individuals from different countries of origin are present. Language differences mean that optimal evangelist are from the same culture as individuals who are targets of evangelism. In the pluralistic United States culture, most effective evangelists come from community cultures rather than affluent and/or predominantly White cultures.

My nephew took high school and college Spanish courses anticipating that he would travel to South America for his two-year mission. Despite his fluency in Spanish, when he arrived in Venezuela he was required to spend 3-4 months in an intensive-language school. The Spanish in Venezuela was different from the Spanish students learned in high schools and colleges in the United States.

Ideally, our churches embrace individuals of different color and different subcultures. That way when church-based individuals reach out as evangelists, they do so in racially and culturally appropriate ways.

In the present chapter and the preceding one, we read about judgement falling on the Earth, nations, and individuals. We learn that Noah and family were the only people faithful in his time period. We rejoice that they were saved despite the worldwide flood.

Notice, despite Noah's drunkenness after the flood, God didn't punish him, or the *Bible* didn't record the punishment. In the 21st century, when ongoing drunkenness is a problem for evangelists, their drunken behavior, a moral failing, disqualifies them for the evangelist role.

Sometime after the flood, perhaps Nimrod ruled in the Shinar Plain, In these days humankind decided they wanted to access God, i.e., to meet and talk with God or to wage war against God. The humans worked on a tower designed to reach the heavens. God looked at the Tower, assessed their motivation, and confounded the language of the people.

Trying to reach God isn't a bad objective in and of itself. Christians, particularly evangelist, want to access God to make themselves better servants of God. Perhaps, in this story what went disastrously wrong was motivations of Tower builders.

From this *Bible* episode and various legends, evangelists can learn that they must look at their motivations for telling individuals about Jesus. If those motivations are set in obedience to Jesus, their motives are consistent with those of God. But, what if an evangelist's motives aren't consistent with the sovereignty of God? Three less than ideal motivations for being an evangelist are:

- Acclaim. Getting praise from fellow Christians for the good they do.
- Wealth. Many evangelists have radio and television programs which have made them wealthy individuals.
- Ego. Reporting to a board of directors or a congregation how many "souls" they led to Jesus.

Each Christian must look at their individual motivations for enacting their Jesus-centered role as an evangelist.

Points to Ponder

1. Was the Tower of Babel and God's subsequent confounding of languages truth or legend? What are reasons for your answer?

2. What is the take-away message from the Tower of Babel episode in the *Bible*?

3. What are your motivations for being an evangelist?

4. To whom are you qualified to be an evangelist? Remember evangelism is more than just words.

5. The notion of Nephilim and beings invisible to the naked eye, i.e. jinn, has fascinated humankind for millennia. Do you believe there were/are beings on earth? Will they be present in the new heaven and earth in Revelations 21 and 22? How are they pertinent to the evangelical message?

6. Go back through the chapter, noting all legends, beliefs, traditions from any source, i.e., Islam, Mormons, Jewish/Israelites, unknown, etc. Have any of these beliefs crept into the Christian faith?

SECTION B

ANCIENT ANCESTORS

The fathers and mothers of Israelites (now known as Jews) were called "Patriarchs" and "Matriarchs." *Bible* lore named three patriarchs: Abraham, Isaac, and Jacob (Israel). Their wives and concubines are the Matriarchs. <u>Muslims</u> and <u>Mormons</u> name the patriarchs "prophets." In these religions/faiths, the patriarch/prophets include Abraham, Isaac, Ishmael, Jacob, and Joseph.

In Section B, I named Joseph a Patriarch although the *Bible* doesn't include him. Joseph's actions kept Israelites alive during a famine by moving them to Egypt.

<u>Mormons</u> believe the King James version of the *Bible*; thus, they believe in Abraham, Isaac, Jacob, and Joseph. The *Book of Mormon* describes a man who meets the criteria for a Patriarch, but isn't in

Genesis. This man is Lehi. In the *Book of Mormon*, Lehi is a Hebrew prophet who led his followers to a promised land in the western hemisphere in approximately 600 BCE.

*****

Abram/Abraham (Chapter 7), the son of Terah, was a 10th generation offspring of Noah. The scroll on the next page has legends about Terah. Abraham had two brothers, Nahor and Haran. Abraham married his half-sister, Sarai/Sarah. Throughout the sections on patriarchs, I use the names Abraham for Abram/Abraham and Sarah for Sarai/Sarah.

In this introduction to Section B, legends about Abraham occurred prior to God telling Abraham to travel to Canaan. Notice one legend on the next page about a tzohar.

An <u>Israelite</u> historian wrote that Abraham confronted King Nimrod while Abraham lived in Mesopotamia. King Nimrod had declared himself a god. Abraham told Nimrod to stop worshiping idols. Nimrod had Abraham thrown into a fiery furnace (*Qur'ān* 37:83-99; 29:16-27). Abraham walked from the furnace unharmed.

<u>Israelite/Jewish</u> legends claim that because Abraham and Sarah had no children, Abraham acted as father to his nephew, Lot, after Haran died. Several authors averred that Abraham adopted Lot. *Bible* lore doesn't substantiate this adoption.

Abraham (Chapter 7) was 75 years-of-age when he left Haran with his wife, Sarah, Lot, servants, and livestock. The group went to Canaan (Genesis 12:4).

Terah, Abraham's Father

Varied Sources

Terah lived in Ur, Mesopotamia. The Qur'ān teaches that Terah's occupation was creating idols. Terah's family worshiped many deities.

Another legend claimed that Terah was the Captain of Nimrod's guard.

Terah left Ur, planning to travel to Canaan, however, stopped in Haran. Both Ur and Haran were centers for worship of Sin (Nanna). Perhaps, Terah felt comfortable in a city that worshiped a Mesopotamian deity.

Terah died in Haran. The family remained there until God told Abraham to travel to a country God would show him.

Abraham and the Tzohar

Legend –
Source Unknown

Legend says that Abraham wore a glowing jewel (tzohar) around his neck.

Originally, the jewel belonged to Adam. It came to Abraham by way of Noah.

The light given off by the tzohar was like sunlight. It illuminated the entire world. The glowing jewel healed all persons who looked at it.

Abraham used the jewel to study the motion of stars. He became a master astrologer.

At the moment Abraham died, the jewel flew up to heaven. God took the jewel and hung it on the orbit of the sun.

Isaac was heir of Abraham and Sarah (Chapter 8). Overall, little about Isaac stands out.

Offspring of Jacob (Chapter 9) were identified as the Children of Israel (Jacob's later name). Jacob's patriarchal status is more related to the number (12) of sons he sired rather than to his moral stature.

Joseph was the first of Jacob's sons to go to Egypt (Chapter 10). His move wasn't voluntary. His older brothers sold Joseph as a slave to a trade caravan heading to Egypt. If Jacob was remembered for his lack of character, Joseph reminds us that some good guys win in the end.

*****

So what do we as evangelists learn from these ancestral fathers and mothers? After all, most of us aren't Jews so technically Israelites Patriarchs and Matriarchs aren't our biological ancestors. The answer is related to faith. Patriarchs and Matriarchs are ancestors in the faith. We learn from their behavior, whether that behavior is admirable or deplorable.

The Patriarchs and Matriarchs give us ideas for evangelism and ideas to avoid when evangelizing. Some of their behaviors we want to mimic; others we want to avoid at all costs. Perhaps, Sarah was an excellent, knowledgeable woman, but I never want to emulate her behavior.

Further, as you will read in the next four chapters, myriads of legends surround the lives of Patriarchs and Matriarchs. Some seem to make sense; some don't. Evangelists interact with multi-cultural individuals. For the evangelist knowing some multicultural beliefs, to include legends, can't be overstated.

7

Abraham and Sarah

According to *Bible* lore (Genesis 12:5-6), Abraham traveled southwest from Haran into Canaan. In Canaan, Abraham's first stop was near Shechem at the great tree of Moreh (possibly a terebinth, *Pistacia palaestina*). There, God appeared to Abraham and repeated that he would give the land to Abraham and Abraham's offspring.

In response, Abraham built an altar and made a sacrifice to God. Likely, Abraham thanked God for his safe journey to Canaan. Possibly, Abraham subtly reminded God that he obeyed God and came to Canaan. God needed to keep his promise and give Abraham children.

In the *Qur'ān*, Abraham was a messenger and prophet from Allah. He was the ancestor of the Ishmaelite Arabs. Muslims believe Abraham and his son Ishmael built the first house of worship on earth. Abraham eradicated idol worship in both the Arabian peninsula and in Canaan. The Islamic holy day Eid-al-adha is celebrated in memory of Abraham. By tradition, Muhammad, the most important prophet is from the bloodline of Abraham. In the *Qur'ān* Allah calls people to follow Abraham's religion (*Qur'ān* 3:95). Abraham is named a friend of God.

The *Book of Mormon* claims that descendants of Abraham inherit the covenant God made with Abraham. The covenant includes both the blessings and obligations. When Jesus visited the Americas, he told people there that the Abrahamic covenant applied to them

Abraham camped in several places in Canaan, then travelled to Egypt to escape a famine in Canaan (Genesis 12:10). Israelite legend claimed that this famine was the second great famine God sent. The first was when God cursed the ground because of Adam and Eve's rebellion against him.

Sarah

Sarah was the first wife of Abraham (*Bible*). Abraham loved Sarah. They had one son, Isaac. Sarah was beautiful and independent. She was confident and acted on her opinions.

In the *Qur'ān*, Sarah had a lesser role than in the *Bible*; she is named only twice. Because angels spoke to Sarah, she is called *muhaddatha*, a title given to prophets and highly meritorious individuals. Some Muslim writers are critical of Sarah because of her treatment of Hagar and role in expelling Ishmael, Abraham's son, and Hagar from the family camp.

Egypt Episode

According to an ancient Israelite/Jewish legend, Abraham didn't have intercourse with Sarah for the first 50 years of their marriage. If this legend is true, it could explain why Sarah was childless most of their married life. Further, Abraham never noticed how beautiful Sarah was until they were on their way to Egypt. Abraham saw Sarah's reflection in water and was overcome by her beauty.

Abraham believed that Egyptian border soldiers would kill him if they thought beautiful Sarah was his wife. Then, soldiers would take Sarah to Pharaoh. Abraham put Sarah in a casket, thinking a casket would pass unopened into Egypt. Unfortunately, soldiers insisted on opening the casket.

Soldiers saw Sarah's beauty. They took her to Pharaoh. When Pharaoh questioned Sarah, she named Abraham her brother, not her husband. Notice, in this legend, unlike in the *Bible*, Sarah rather than Abraham told the lie that Sarah was Abraham's sister. Sarah was placed in Pharaoh's harem. Pharaoh heaped treasure upon Abraham because he was Sarah's brother.

Jewish legend says that when Pharaoh tried to touch Sarah, an invisible angel struck him. Despite several attempts, Pharaoh couldn't touch Sarah. Then, God struck Pharaoh, his nobles, and servants with leprosy. Pharaoh consulted Egyptian priests and soothsayers. They told Pharaoh that the leprosy occurred because he took Abraham's wife into his harem.

Horrified that he claimed another man's wife, Pharaoh returned Sarah to Abraham without demanding his gifts back (Genesis 12:17-20). When Abraham and Sarah returned to Canaan, Hagar, a slave that Pharaoh gave Sarah, went with them. One ancient <u>Arab</u> legend recorded that Hagar was a princess, the daughter of Egypt's Pharaoh.

Returning to Canaan, Abraham settled at the great trees of Marme (Genesis 13:18). The great trees at Marme were likely oak trees (*Quercus calliprinos*). Abraham settled on a Hebron hill around 1720 BCE. The area later became Hebron ("friend").

Ishmael

As time progressed, Abraham and Sarah had no children. Likely, both asked how they were going to be ancestors of a nation when they were childless.

Sarah determined to solve the problem using traditions of Mesopotamian culture (*Bible*). Remember, Abraham and Sarah's ancestors were from Ur in Mesopotamia. They were aware of Mesopotamian traditions whereby a wife could offer another woman to her husband for the purpose of bearing children. Sarah persuaded Abraham to take her Egyptian slave woman, Hagar, as a secondary wife (concubine).

The *Bible* recorded that Abraham sired a son (Ishmael) with Hagar. When Ishmael was a teen, Sarah birthed a son, Isaac. At Isaac's weaning ceremony, Hagar and Ishmael mocked Isaac. Sarah told Abraham to expel Hagar and Ishmael from his camp (Genesis 21:8-13).

Abraham was devastated at Sarah's demand, but God agreed with Sarah. Read the scroll on the next page to understand why Sarah may have been powerful enough to make the demand that Ishmael be expelled from Abraham's camp.

In Islamic tradition Abraham traveled with Hagar and Ishmael into the desert. As Abraham walked away from Hagar, she asked Abraham if God directed him to abandon her and Ishmael. Abraham responded affirmatively. Hagar said, "Then God will provide for us."

In the desert, Ishmael cried for water. Hagar went in search of water, but could find none. Hagar asked God's help. According to Arab legend, God sent the angel Gabriel to assist Hagar. At Gabriel's direction, Hagar picked up Ishmael. When she lifted Ishmael, Hagar noticed that Ishmael's feet scratched the soil. There, a spring of water bubbled up. The water formed the Zamzam Well. The Well became a holy site and base of the Islamic holy city of Mecca in Saudi Arabia.

Ishmael sired 12 sons and an unknown number of daughters. The 12 sons were fathers of Arab nations. One daughter married Esau. Ishmael was the first and most significant son of Abraham.

Keturah

Bible readers think of Sarah as Abraham's wife; however, after Sarah died Abraham took another wife

Sarah as Priestess

Mesopotamian legend

The *Bible* identified Sarah as beautiful, hospitable, and obedient to her husband. Yet, in several *Bible* episodes, Sarah acted decisive and independently of Abraham's leadership.

One legend contended that Sarah was a priestess in ancient Mesopotamia. Legend advances that priestesses were a privileged class of women. A priestess played a greater role than her husband in directing the family's life.

As a priestess, Sarai had authority to direct Abraham to mate with Hagar and expel Hagar and Ishmael from Abraham's camp.

(Genesis 25:1-4). Her name was Keturah. In the *Bible*, one reference named Keturah as Abraham's wife; another named her a concubine (secondary wife). The *Book of Jubilees* (19:11) claimed that originally Keturah was one of Abraham's household servants.

Rashi (Rabbi Solomon ben Isaac), one of the most influential Israelite/Jewish commentators in history, wrote that Keturah was Hagar, who Abraham had married more than 50 years earlier. Hagar bore Abraham's firstborn, Ishmael. In this legend, Isaac was the matchmaker. After Sarah died, Isaac travelled to Hagar and brought her back to Abraham's home. Isaac had positive feelings towards Hagar and considered her worthy to again be his father's wife.

Why was Hagar named Keturah? There were two reasons. First, Hagar was good and pure like *ketoret*, the incense on the altar in the Muslim Holy Temple. Second, during the approximately 50 years Abraham and Hagar were apart, Hagar never cohabited with a man. She remained faithful and true to Abraham. In the Aramaic language, *keturah* means "bound." Hagar remained bound to Abraham throughout all those years.

Deaths

Although about 10 years younger than Abraham, Sarah died (127 years) before Abraham (*Bible*). When Sarah died, Abraham bought a tree-covered field (Genesis 23:17-20) at Machpelah near Hebron. At one end was a cave where Abraham placed Sarah's dead body.

A <u>Jewish</u> mystical teaching claimed that Adam and Eve were already buried in the Machpelah cave. The first time Abraham entered it, he saw a light. Adam and Eve's graves were revealed to Abraham. Adam was there and alive. When Adam saw Abraham, happiness filled Adam's expression. Abraham asked Adam if there was an opening for Sarah and him to be buried there.

Adam answered Abraham that the All-Mighty buried him there. Since Adam's burial, Adam was hidden from human eyes until Abraham lived. From that time onward, the covenant God made with Adam and humanity would exist through Abraham. Another <u>legend</u> was that the cave at Machpelah was an entrance to the Garden of Eden. Adam was buried there to be close to Eden, his original home.

Abraham lived 175 years. During his lifetime, he gave gifts to Keturah's sons and sent them from his camp. Abraham made it clear that Isaac was his heir. The *Bible* recorded (Genesis 25:9) that Isaac and Ishmael buried Abraham in the cave of Machpelah.

Three couples were buried in the Machpelah cave: Abraham and Sarah, Isaac and Rebekah, and Jacob and Leah. If this mystical <u>Jewish</u> teaching is correct, then four couples were buried in the cave. Adam and Eve's bodies were there.

What About Evangelism?

Abraham believed God. Abraham's faith in what God told him was credited to Abraham as righteousness (Genesis 15:6).

When Christians are asked, "Who was the greatest evangelist in the *Bible*?" many respond with Jesus, John the Baptist, or St. Paul. When asked "Who was the greatest evangelist in the Old Testament?" most give a blank stare. After some thinking, often their response is Moses or Jonah.

I believe that Abraham was the greatest evangelist in the Old Testament and arguably in the *Bible* after Jesus. My rationale is that Abraham heard the voice of God. He believed in a God few, if any, other humankind recognized. Abraham obeyed God.

As Abraham journeyed around Canaan, likely he was asked why he was there. Why did Abraham leave Haran? Few Mesopotamians left the land where they were born. Certainly, few traveled to Canaan, an obscure region of the ancient near East. In these meetings, Abraham revealed that God led him to Canaan. Abraham gave his personal testimony of obedience to God.

Abraham took the reality of a single God throughout Canaan. In his travels Abraham demonstrated that God moves toward individuals. God, in Abraham, moved toward Canaanites. Like Abraham, evangelists go into harvest fields. In these fields (their community, their mission field) God has already touched some targets. God prepared target's souls to be open to the message carried by an evangelist. This preparation by God is often called God's prevenient grace. It's a grace of preparation from God in a target's life so the target is ready and willing to accept an evangelist's message. Evangelist realize that when they go into the fields of harvest to tell individual targets about Jesus they are part of a long or short list of individuals who have gone before them.

Abraham's conduct when purchasing the field of Machpelah from Ephron showed observers a man who followed an ethical God and was himself an ethical man. The story setting would have been at the entrance of a Hittite town near the Machpelah field. Abraham refused Ephron's (the Hittites) offer to gift Abraham the land. Abraham insisted on paying for it. In this story we see Abraham's testimony, his right thinking as God's servant.

Likely, Abraham and fellow travelers didn't think of themselves as evangelists. But they were. In their obedience, they were proponents of God, even when they didn't mention God's name. In the 21st century, the greatest way to evangelize is to obey God. We tell others about God in our obedience to him, i.e., go into world, preach the gospel, live a moral life, etc.

Once, I heard a great preacher say: "Preach the gospel to everyone, use words if necessary." The best way evangelists tell others about Jesus Christ is being obedient to God's commands and the way they live. Admittedly, sometimes it's easier to tell others what to believe, than to exhibit that same belief.

Evangelists are scrutinized by individuals inside and outside of the faith to see if their behavior matches their words. After about the first five years in Canaan, wherever Abraham and family went people knew about him. Canaanites heard that Abraham worshiped only one God. Abraham claimed this God was the one true God. Their idols were worthless.

Points to Ponder

1. How could you make the argument that Abraham was the first evangelist?

2. Who do you think told Pharaoh that Sarah was Abraham's sister? Does it matter to the evangelist's purpose who told the lie?

3. What is the biblical evidence to support legends that when Abraham buried Sarah in the Machpelah cave, he found Adam and Eve buried there? Do you think this particular legend has merit?

4. How is the non-verbal behavior of an evangelist important?

5. Why is it important that an evangelist be ethical?

6. If Ishmael remained Abraham's heir, would there be Arab nations and an Islamic religion? Why or why not? How do events as long as 4000 years ago impact your message as an evangelist?

8

Isaac and Rebekah

Do you know the <u>American</u> proverb, "Like father, like son." That proverb contends that a son mimics the behavior of his father. Isaac's life demonstrated that he was like his father, Abraham — Isaac loved his wife, worked hard, and dug wells for access to water. Similar to Abraham, Isaac pretended his wife was a sister to protect himself in a foreign land. God blessed Isaac and he prospered.

Abraham and Sarah were overjoyed to have a son (Isaac). He was the son God promised them; the son through whom the entire world would be blessed. Despite this *Bible* lore, there are extra-biblical perspectives on Isaac's birth. See the scroll on the next page for Isaac's birth <u>legends</u>. Isaac had one wife and no concubines or secondary wives. Isaac married Rebekah, his cousin.

Sacrifice

God commanded Abraham to take Isaac to Mount Moriah and sacrifice him as a burnt offering to God (Genesis 22:1-19). Abraham didn't hesitate or question God's command. Nor did Abraham tell Sarah God's order. I imagine Abraham kept this information from Sarah to protect her feelings. Alternatively, Abraham thought that Sarah would

Isaac's Birth Legends

Jewish Tradition

Philo, a Jewish thinker in Alexandria, Egypt, believed the Torah was an allegory and interpreted many episodes. He postulated: Sarah was a virgin when Isaac was conceived. Isaac's wasn't Abraham's son, but God's son. Isaac was conceived and born on the same day.

The day Isaac was born a splendor filled the earth. Such a splendor wasn't seen since before Adam and Eve's rebellion. It will only be seen again in the world to come. Isaac was so in tune with the power behind the cosmos, that he typified joy.

strenuously object to God's direction and her objection would influence his actions. A scroll on the next page describes some legendary interactions Sarah had with Satan while Abraham and Isaac were on the Mount Moriah trek.

On Mount Moriah, Abraham built an altar, arranged wood on it, and tied Isaac on the altar. Abraham picked up his knife to sacrifice Isaac. At the last minute, an angel told Abraham to not kill Isaac. The angel commended Abraham's willingness to obey God.

By Israelite tradition the site of Abraham's planned sacrifice of Isaac is the location of Solomon's temple.

A Christian tradition is that Christ's crucifixion site and the site of Abraham's planned sacrifice of Isaac are the same.

In Islam Ishmael, not Isaac, was the son that God told Abraham to sacrifice. I am amazed at the differences in opinion between Judeo-Christians and Muslims about which son was the pending sacrifice. Christians are firm that the son was Isaac, while Muslims are equally firm that it was Ishmael. Perhaps, Abraham's willingness to obey God and sacrifice a son is more important than which son he was prepared to offer.

In the ancient near East, humankind believed that the more an individual valued a sacrifice (made to a god), the more merit the individual derived by

Satan Confronts Sarah

Unknown Source

Satan came to Sarah disguised as an old man. Satan told Sarah that Abraham sacrificed Isaac.

Sarah cried bitterly, but soon comforted herself with the thought that Abraham offered the sacrifice at God's command.

Sarah started walking from Beersheba to Hebron. She asked each individual she met if he/she knew in which direction Abraham went.

Satan came again in his human shape to Sarah. Satan told Sarah that Isaac wasn't sacrificed. Isaac was alive and would return home soon.

On hearing this good news, Sarah died of joy near Hebron.

making it. Abraham's willingness to offer his son showed great loyalty and obedience to God.

A Wife for Isaac

According to the *Bible*, Abraham wanted Isaac to have a wife so his line would continue; however, Abraham didn't want Isaac to marry a Canaanite woman. An aged Abraham gave a senior servant (believed to be Eliezer) the task of traveling to Abraham's hometown, Nahor in Paddan Aram, and bringing back a wife for Isaac (Genesis 24:1-4). Multiple myths/legends surround acquiring Isaac's wife.

Eliezer traveled by camel caravan. The caravan carried valuable gifts for the family of Isaac's wife-to-be (Genesis 24:10). Normally, the trek from Canaan to Paddan Aram took as long as 17 days. An Israelite/Jewish legend said that Eliezer made the trip from Canaan to Paddan Aram in three hours; and the return trip from Paddan Aram to Canaan in three hours. The earth reconfigured itself so Eliezer could travel across it in a short time. Most of us don't believe this legend. Certainly, modern day scientists wouldn't support it.

Eliezer arrived at a well near Nahor in Paddan Aram. There, he met Rebekah (Genesis 24:15-21). Bethuel, the youngest son of Nahor and Milcah (Genesis 24:47), was Rebekah's father.

One ancient legend stated that Bethuel was a king and Rebekah a princess; however, there is little if any other information to support this legend. What is undisputable is that Bethuel and Rebekah were polytheists. They worshiped many gods. Consistent with their culture, the family had small idols to gods throughout their home.

The *Bible* recorded that at Bethuel's home, Eliezer requested that Rebekah travel with him back to Canaan immediately and become Isaac's wife. The family agreed. Conceivably, they were influenced by the wealth that Eliezer gave to their family.

Many Christian scholars believe that Isaac was around 40 and Rebekah a mid-teen when they married. Jewish sages offered alternative ages. See scroll on next page for legends about their ages.

Rebekah

An Israelite/Jewish legend claimed that when Isaac took Rebekah to the tent of his dead mother (Sarah), a cloud appeared over the tent. The cloud was visible over the tent during Sarah's life and vanished with her death. The same cloud reappeared when Rebekah entered the tent. The cloud miraculously appeared each day except on the Sabbath. The door of Rebekah's tent were opened to the needy, as they were in Sarah's day.

Love in Isaac's marriage is assumed; but perhaps, that assumption is wrong. The *Bible* recorded that Isaac loved Rebekah (Genesis 24:67). The *Bible* didn't

Ages at Marriage

Jewish Sages

Jewish sages wrote that Rebekah was as young as 3 years-of-age when Abraham's servant brought her to Canaan. That is the reason Rebekah traveled with her nurse, Deborah. Supposedly, at this young age, Rebekah was free from deception prevalent in her family.

Other sages wrote that Rebekah was 10 and still others that she was 14 when she married Isaac.

Sages proposed that Isaac's age was 40 when he married Rebekah. In this legend, Isaac was 26 when Abraham bound him on the Mount Moriah altar and when Sarah died.

Other sages proposed that Isaac was in his 40s when the event on Mount Moriah occurred.

record that Rebekah loved Isaac. The first time the *Bible* identified that Rebekah loved anyone was her love for her son, Jacob (Genesis 25:28).

One scholar boldly averred that ancestors of Israelites should be identified as Abraham, Rebekah (Isaac's wife), and Jacob rather than Abraham, Isaac, and Jacob. In this view, Rebekah played a more prominent role than her husband in episodes during Isaac's life.

Isaac's Deception

In the *Bible*, Canaan experienced a famine (Genesis 26:1-6). Isaac took his family to Gerar, a region in Canaan controlled by Philistines, where food was available. There, Isaac told the Philistine king that the beautiful Rebekah was his sister. Isaac didn't believe that God would protect him from the Philistine king just as Abraham didn't believe that God would protect him from the Egyptian Pharaoh. When the Philistine king learned of Isaac's deception, he returned Rebekah to Isaac along with a large sum of money, ostensibly to cover Rebekah's shame.

An Israelite legend asserted that Isaac introduced the practice of giving a tithe to the poor while he lived in Gerar. God was so pleased with Isaac's practice that Isaac's land yielded one hundred times more than expected. The Philistines were envious of Isaac's wealth. The king asked Isaac to leave Gerar. Eventually, Isaac and family settled east of Gerar in the Beersheba area of Canaan.

Isaac's Sons

After 20 years of marriage, Rebekah birthed twin boys (Genesis 25:24-26). The first-born was Esau and the second-born Jacob. As first-born, Esau was destined to be Isaac's heir. The *Bible* recorded that Isaac preferred Esau while Rebekah preferred Jacob (Genesis 27:27-28). The *Bible* gave no reason for either preference.

The *Bible* included little information about the twin's childhood, however, legends supplied information. Israelite/Jewish sages taught that Esau was an idol worshiper while Jacob worshiped God. Esau had Isaac convinced that he piously worshiped God. Rebekah had a clearer vision of Esau. She knew that Esau was neither pious, nor worshiped God. Her insight into her sons' characters caused Rebekah to love Jacob, more than she loved Esau.

According to legends, Esau and Jacob hunted men; but their motives for hunting differed. Esau hunted men to turn them to idolatry. In contrast, Jacob hunted men to turn them to God.

A legend recorded that Esau killed Nimrod; however, likely, Nimrod was dead by the time Esau lived. According to the *Bible*, Esau married three women, two Canaanite women and a daughter of Ishmael (Genesis 28:6-9).

Isaac Deceived

As Isaac aged, his eyesight diminished (Genesis 27:1) Three <u>legends</u> suggested reasons for Isaac's sight loss. First, Esau's wives burnt incense to their gods in Isaac's home. Incense smoke and particulates promoted Isaac's loss of vision. Second, when Abraham bound Isaac on the altar for sacrifice, angel's tears fell on Isaac's eyes and weakened them. Third, Isaac brought God's wrath on himself because he preferred Esau over Jacob. Isaac's punishment was losing his sight.

When Isaac was old and couldn't see, he wanted to confer the family blessing on Esau, the oldest son. Isaac asked Esau to hunt for wild game and prepare a tasty dish for him (Genesis 27:1-30). <u>Legend</u> contends that Esau expected to readily find a deer to make Isaac's favorite food. Unfortunately, Satan went with Esau on the hunt. Esau found and bound deer, then went in search for more wild game. Satan liberated each deer. When Esau returned to the spot where deer was tied, they were gone. This process occurred many times and resulted in Esau being later then expected to make a savory dish for Isaac.

In the interval, Rebekah enacted a plan to secure Isaac's blessing for Jacob (*Bible*). Following Rebekah's instructions, Jacob dressed in Esau's clothes and covered his hands with goat's skin to make himself hairy to Isaac's touch. Jacob gave Isaac food which Rebekah prepared. Jacob passed the food off as wild game. The deception worked. Isaac gave

Jacob the family blessing which rightfully belonged to Esau.

The ancient *Epic of Gilgamesh* showed similarities with this *Bible* episode, for example, Gilgamesh is described as smooth skinned and a smooth talker similar to Jacob. In contrast, Gilgamesh's opponent, Enkidu, was a hairy man like Esau. Gilgamesh's mother gave him wise advice just as Jacob's mother (Rebekah) gave Jacob advice. Likely, the Mesopotamian Gilgamesh epic preceded this Isaacson's episode by a few centuries. It's feasible the *Epic of Gilgamesh* influenced this *Bible* episode.

Isaac and Rebekah's Deaths

Isaac was the longest-lived Israelite Patriarch, living about 180 years. Although Rebekah was dead, Isaac was alive when Jacob returned to the family home after living in Paddan Aram and in the Bethel area. When Rebekah died, Isaac buried her in the cave of Machpelah. When Isaac died, Jacob and Esau buried him in the cave of Machpelah (Genesis 35:29).

What about Evangelism?

When Isaac went to Gerar, Isaac told the king that Rebekah was his sister rather than acknowledging her as his wife.

So many legends, so many beliefs from different faiths, so many lies in Isaac's life. What can we glean from these stories that evangelists can use to promote belief in the true God? First, we must look at the context of the story. Isaac, Rebekah, Esau, and Jacob are a family. In the ancient near East, family had first claim on an individual's life, before personal goals, wants, desires, and worship of gods.

According to Bishop Robert Barron, when we accept the God of Israel and Jesus as Christ, we reprioritize what is important to us, including family, gods, culture, political party, artistic form, and ideas other than the God of Israel and his Son, Jesus Christ. For an evangelist, powerful family ties must give way to the mission of telling others about the redeeming power of Jesus. Jesus said that nothing can come before following him (Luke 14:33).

When I contemplated the lore, legend, and lies about Isaac and Rebekah, my thoughts went to the number of outright lies and deliberate disinformation that was shown in this family. Rebekah's lies and behavior make her a questionable wife and mother. Both Abraham (preceding chapter) and Isaac lied to the Philistine king about their true relationship with their wife.

Is it acceptable for an evangelist to lie for a good cause, such as convincing an individual to accept Jesus as Redeemer? My personal belief is that it's not. Included in that belief is to not lie about behavior of people or events, even by implication.

When evangelizing, it's never appropriate to bash beliefs of other religions. Recently, I was at a community dinner. In casual conversation, individuals were discussing a minority faith. Some conversationalists made sceptical faces when discussing the faith. I am concerned about these types of facial expressions. They could alienate some individuals in the group. There are ways besides words to convey a message of disdain.

Some Christian theologians assert that Jacob deceiving Isaac over the issue of the family blessing was God's punishment to Isaac for deceiving the king of Gerar. Some events in Genesis, such as this one, aren't germane to telling others the story of Jesus' work on the cross. When possible, don't go there in your evangelism. If your targeted individual brings up the problematic behavior of a *Bible* character, your response could be that the *Bible* doesn't describe only idealized behavior, but real-life actions of *Bible* men and women.

According to Israelite/Jewish legend when Isaac was in Gerar he instituted the practice of tithing, giving a percent of his profits to the poor. Maybe, Isaac started the practice of tithing, however, there is no concrete information one way or the other. If true, certainly Isaac's behavior is admirable.

A chapter legend claimed that Jacob hunted men (women and children, too). Jacob wanted to convert them from worship of false gods to worship of the true God. Although this legend is likely false, the lesson is superlative. Evangelists hunt men, women, and children for the purpose of converting them to worship the true God. Many of them worship false gods or no god.

Points to Ponder

1. Why did Abraham not want a Canaanite wife for Isaac? Was Abraham prejudice? How can an evangelist be prejudice?

2. Some theologians believe that Rebekah is more worthy than Isaac to be named in the list of Israelite ancestors. What do you think based on material in this chapter and more importantly in the *Bible*? Why do you think that Rebekah's name wasn't included? Should evangelists make Rebekah a central part of their message?

3. Give examples of when you felt a need to help God with his plans, even plans of how to be an evangelist. How did that work out?

4. What is the significance of Rebekah loving one of the three men in her life more than the other two? How can favoritism impact evangelistic activities?

5. What is tithing? Should tithing be promoted in evangelism?

6. Think deeply about legends (Christian, Muslim, and Israelite/Jewish) in this chapter to include Isaac's almost-sacrifice on Mount Moriah. How should these happenings influence or not influence the evangelist's message?

9

JACOB AND WIVES

The *Bible* recorded that as Isaac's sons (Esau and Jacob) grew, Jacob envied Esau's birthright (Genesis 25:19-34). The birthright belonged to the eldest son (Esau) in a family. He was named heir to the father (Isaac). Through unloving and duplicitous acts, Jacob stole the birthright and blessing which rightfully belonged to Esau.

In the Mormon faith, Jacob obtained the family birthright over his brother Esau. Jacob's in the covenant, while Esau despised his birthright and married outside the covenant. Remember, Esau married two Canaanite women and one daughter of Ishmael. Kept the commandments and is exalted on a throne in heaven, in company with Abraham and Isaac

Esau was angry at Jacob because of Jacob's deceit; he threatened to kill Jacob (Genesis 27:41). Jacob left Isaac's camp for the ostensible reason that he was going to his mother's (Rebekah's) family in Paddan Aram to find a wife. Likely, Jacob left the family home to escape Esau's anger.

Think back to the *Bible* story where Eliezer was sent by Abraham to Paddan Aram to find a wife for Isaac. Eliezer traveled in a caravan with 10 camels. The camels contained valuable gifts for Isaac's wife to-be and her family. Now, imagine how Isaac and Rebekah sent Jacob off to obtain a wife. Jacob took gifts to Rebekah's family in Paddan Aram, particularly if he was seeking a wife. Yet, when Jacob arrived in Paddan Aram, he had to work seven years to claim a bride. What happened? The *Bible* gives no information.

Attempts on Jacob's Life

Legend recorded that Esau made two attempts to kill Jacob after Jacob left Isaac's camp to travel to Paddan Aram. In the first legend, Esau sent his son, Eliphaz, to kill Jacob and take Jacob's belongings. Eliphaz robbed Jacob of gold, silver, food, camels, etc.; however, God caused Eliphaz to spare Jacob's life. When Eliphaz returned to Esau with the riches, Esau took them and reprimanded Eliphaz for not killing Jacob.

The second legend contends that Esau determined to kill Jacob himself to be sure the deed was done. He left home and caught up with Jacob while Jacob was bathing in a hot spring. Esau and his men surrounded the hot spring, covering all exits. Miraculously, God opened a new exit from the hot spring and Jacob escaped.

A Night at Bethel

Jacob's journey from Canaan to Paddan Aram took many days. One evening, Jacob stopped in the Bethel area, went to sleep, and had a dream (Genesis 28:10-22, *Bible*). In the dream Jacob saw a stairway between earth and heaven with angels ascending and descending on it. Above the stairway stood God. God told Jacob he was the God of Abraham and Isaac. He would be Jacob's God. Then, God reaffirmed the promises he made to Abraham:

- God would give Jacob the land on which he slept.
- Jacob would have multiple descendants.
- All Earth's peoples would be blessed through Jacob's offspring.
- God would be with Jacob.
- God would bring Jacob back to Canaan.

The story of Jacob seeing a ladder that reached to heaven is familiar to most Judeo-Christians. An Israelite/Jewish legend evolved around the episode. In it, Jacob was an archangel, the first minister before God. He was the first living being God gave life. Jacob's heavenly name was Israel.

When Israel descended to earth and became Jacob, he forgot his divine origin. God tried to remind Jacob who he was by sending him the dream of the ladder reaching between earth and heaven. Angels went up the staircase to heaven and encouraged heavenly angels to descend the staircase to see Jacob, the pious.

After Jacob arrived in Paddan Aram, he stayed with Laban, Rebekah's brother (Genesis 29:13-30). It's possible that Jacob brought no wealth with him. In this scenario, the legend of Eliphaz robbing his uncle has some validity.

Superstitions

Jacob married two of Laban's daughters, Leah and Rachel. Jacob loved Rachel, but didn't love Leah. See the scroll on the next page for an explanations of the value of both Leah and Rachel to the Israelite nation.

A *Bible* story of mandrakes began with Leah's oldest son, Reuben, bringing mandrake roots to Leah (Genesis 30:14-24). Rachel saw the mandrakes and proposed a trade — Jacob can sleep with Leah that night in exchange for the mandrakes. Leah became pregnant after spending the night with Jacob. She bore Jacob a fifth son, Issachar. Rachel didn't become pregnant from acquiring and in some fashion using the mandrakes.

Many Westerners can't make much sense of this *Bible* story. What do mandrakes have to do with pregnancy? Truthfully, nothing; yet in the ancient near East women believed (<u>superstitiously</u>) that mandrake roots promoted conception. Frequently, thick roots are forked, similar to two legs. Women consumed the mandrake root in minute amounts, cut it into an amulet to wear around the neck, or put the root beneath their bed.

The *Bible* didn't record whether or not Jacob believed his wives' <u>superstition</u> (lie) about the mandrake; however, Jacob had his own superstitious beliefs. Jacob wanted to return to Canaan; but he didn't want to return to Canaan a poor man. Jacob made an agreement with Laban — he would continue to care for Laban's flocks if Laban would give him all the spotted and stripped offspring.

Leah and Rachel

Jewish Sages' Perspective

Leah was the first wife of Jacob and the mother of seven of his children.

Rachel relinquished her destined husband to spare Leah degradation and embarrassment. Rachel allowed her swindling father, Laban, to veil Leah and replace her as Jacob's bride.

Because Leah loved Rachel, Leah prayed that Rachel would have children.

Both women were needed for the children of Israel to achieve their destiny. Moses, Leah's descendant, led the exodus from Egypt. Joshua, Rachel's progeny, led Israelites into the Promised Land.

King Saul was descended from Rachel. King David was descended from Leah.

Superstitiously, Jacob believed that if goats and sheep mated in front of stripped or spotted tree branches, their offspring would be stripped or spotted (Genesis 30:37-45, *Bible*)). Jacob acted on this superstition. Jacob took fresh poplar (*Populus alba*), almond (*Prunus dulcis*), and plane (*Platanus orientalis*) tree branches. He peeled bark from branches so that white streaks and spots showed. Jacob set the pealed branches in front of flocks at water troughs where male and female animals mated. Likely, Jacob's superstition came from folktales of Mesopotamian people.

Return from Paddan Aram

Jacob's return trip from Paddan Aram to Canaan was event-filled. Possibly, the trip took as long as two years. During it, Jacob wrestled with an angel. God changed Jacob's name to Israel (despite Jacob's name change, I continue to use the name "Jacob" throughout the book).

One ancient legend claimed that the celestial being that Jacob wrestled with was Samael, the guardian angel of Esau and another name for Satan. Jacob prevailing over Samuel was prophecy that Jacob would prevail against Esau.

Some ancient scholars believe that the *Bible* story of Jacob wrestling with a celestial being was borrowed from a Mesopotamian epic, *Epic of Gilgamesh*. The Gilgamesh epic was known throughout the ancient near East at the time of Jacob's life. Some common features between the Gilgamesh epic and Jacob's life are listed below:

- Both Jacob and Gilgamesh wrestled with a being that was supernatural.
- In the *Epic of Gilgamesh,* Gilgamesh's antagonist, Enkidu, was created by gods. Jacob's antagonist may have been an angel or even God.
- Gilgamesh was accosted when he was alone.
- The wrestling match was unarmed conflict. It wasn't to death.
- The wrestling match was a rite of passage for both men. Before it Gilgamesh was a harsh, unbearable ruler. After it and a heroic journey, Gilgamesh focused on more worthwhile endeavors. Before the wrestling match Jacob was egocentric, sly, and manipulative. Afterward, Jacob attains the title Patriarch and father of the Children of Israel.

After all these events, God instructed Jacob to go to Bethel, and build an altar to God (Genesis 35:1-5). Before Jacob left the Shechem area, he collected all household idols from his wives and servants. Jacob buried them under the oak (*Quercus calliprinos*) of Shechem.

Jacob's action implied that henceforth he and his family would no longer be polytheists but worship the God of his fathers. Islam, Judaism, and Christianity are the three great monotheistic religions. In all three faiths, burying, destroying, or removing idols from the home is a positive action.

After Bethel, Jacob's family traveled to Isaac's home and was reunited with Isaac. By this time, Rachel was dead and Jacob had twelve sons and one daughter.

Jacob's Favoritism

Just as Isaac and Rebekah had a favorite son, so did Jacob. Jacob loved Joseph more than Leah's sons. Jacob made Joseph "heir" in place of his first-born son, Rueben. Jealous of Jacob's preference of Joseph, his older brothers sold Joseph to Ishmaelites in a trade caravan traveling to Egypt (Genesis 37:28).

Islam Perspective

In Islam Jacob is presented in a much more favorable light than in the *Bible*. According to the *Qur'ān*, Jacob preached the oneness of God. Allah made a covenant with him and made Jacob a faithful leader throughout Jacob's life. The *Qur'ān* mentions that Allah guided Jacob and gave him knowledge, and a tongue of truthfulness. A tongue of truthfulness isn't an attribute Jacob evidences in the *Bible*.

In Islam, Jacob had the gift of knowledge. Jacob never believed that Joseph was dead. Constantly, Jacob prayed that Joseph would be returned to him. Joseph's brothers taunted Jacob for his belief that Joseph was alive and his prayers for Joseph's well-being. In his goodness, Jacob ignored his sons' criticisms.

Jacob's Response to Famine

Years later, Canaan experienced a famine (*Bible*). Jacob sent his sons to Egypt to purchase grain so the family wouldn't starve. Unrecognized by his brothers, Joseph was the Egyptian who sold them grain. Joseph held Simeon in Egypt as a hostage for his brothers to return to Egypt with Benjamin, their youngest brother, and Joseph's only full brother.

When Jacob's family was again on the brink of starvation, Jacob allowed his sons to take Benjamin to Egypt and purchase grain. On the sons' second trip to Egypt, Joseph disclosed himself to his brothers. Eventually, Jacob and family (about 70 persons) moved from Canaan and resettled in Goshen, Egypt under the care of Joseph. This number of individuals who went to Egypt implies that Jacob likely took no, or few, servants with him.

Jacob's Death

In an Israelite/Jewish legend, souls of individuals buried in the Machpelah cave i.e., Adam and Eve, Abraham and Sarah, and Isaac and Rebekah, went to Egypt with Jacob. When souls left the cave, a candle burning in it extinguished.

After Jacob died (approximate age 147), Joseph and brothers took his body to Canaan to be buried in the cave of Machpelah. When Jacob's body was placed in the cave, the candle relit itself. The cave's glory was restored. Israelite/Jewish sages believe the cave will never accept another body.

See the legend about Jacob's burial on the next page. As you read you conclude that animosity between Jacob and Esau that began in childhood continued until after Jacob's death, as long as 120 years.

Jacob's Burial

A Jewish Legend

When Jacob died, he was taken to the cave of Machpelah for burial. There, Esau refused to permit Jacob to be interned in the cave. Esau claimed he had the right to be buried in the cave.

A fight ensued between the children of Esau and Jacob. Forty of Esau's men were killed.

Dan's son, Chushim, grabbed a weapon and swung it at Esau's head. The mighty blow severed Esau's head. Esau's head rolled into the cave of Machpelah. Esau's men took his headless body back to their home. The legend didn't disclose the final location of Esau's body.

Jacob was buried in the cave of Machpelah beside Leah.

What about Evangelism?

Jacob wanted Esau's birthright. Jacob wanted Rachel for a wife rather than Leah. Jacob wanted Joseph as heir rather than Reuben. Jacob wanted large flocks.

In the *Bible*, Jacob was an enthusiastic proponent of no one but himself. He didn't even put his beloved Rachel before his own wants (Genesis 30:1-2). Jacob gave up his integrity, reliability, veracity, and honor to get that title of heir from Isaac. Plus, Jacob want to be rich when he returned to his father's home. Jacob continued bullying, selfish behavior while living in Paddan Aram. What can an evangelist learn from such a character?

An evangelist will encounter individuals that they don't agree with or condone their behavior. Some behaviors, i.e., abuse of children, women, and men, human trafficking, I find appalling. Does God expect me, as an evangelist, to tell human traffickers about Jesus? Yes! Nowhere in the *Bible* does God give me the freedom to decide who I tell about the gospel based on their life choices.

When you determine to be an evangelist to neighbors and workplace friends, they may identify ways that you've acted suboptimal, i.e., deceived, stole paper supplies from the company, became impatient. If these scenarios happen, don't argue, or justify your behavior. Admit your faults and re-direct the conversation to the need for all people to be redeemed including yourself. The evangelist needs a Savior just like everyone else. One of my favorite clergymen, reminded me that we are all recovering sinners. We won't be cured sinners until we enter heaven.

Jacob knew about God, possibly from Abraham and definitely from Isaac most of his childhood, teenage, and young adult years. God spoke with Jacob in a dream on Jacob's way to Paddan Aram; nevertheless likely, Jacob worshiped his wife's idols during his years in Paddan Aram. At a minimum, Jacob accepted his wives' polytheism.

Jacob disregarded his grandfather and father's testimony about God for decades. Finally, Jacob turned to God. Jacob had a direct revelation from God that turned his life around. Most individuals aren't going to get a direct revelation from God. Their revelation will come through an evangelist.

Will you ever have to be an evangelist to a Pastor's offspring, or an individual you know grew up in a Christ-centered family? Yes, you will need to talk about Jesus' redemptive work to individuals like that. Remember, evangelists plant seeds just as Abraham and Isaac planted seeds in Jacob's life. The Holy Spirit gives the increase.

What should an evangelists do when targeted individuals are superstitious? These individuals may even cite Jacob's superstitious actions in attempting to increase his flocks' size. They conclude that because the story is in the *Bible,* it is okay to be superstitious. If this scenario occurs, the evangelist can point out that Jacob's superstitious actions weren't the reason flocks increased in size. God gave the increase in flocks' size because the increase was consistent with God's will.

When encountering superstitions, the first step for the evangelists is to make sure they aren't harboring superstitions themself. Superstitions are subtle. Grandmom Byers had a horseshoe above her door with the prongs pointed down. She believed that the "cold iron" protected her from any evil that entered through her door. Her belief was superstitious. I grew up with it, despite believing in Jesus and God. I didn't know any better and retained some of my childhood superstitions until my faith in God matured. I now know that the way evil is prevented is through the Holy Spirit in us and by extension in the world.

Step two for the evangelist is to be aware of vocabulary. Often, we say, "Good Luck" to another person. Words such as "Good Luck" are such a part of westernized culture, we say them automatically, without thought. Hopefully, no Christian believes in luck. Their faith is in God who causes the rain to fall on the just and unjust. Importantly, superstitious words and actions need to be removed from our vocabulary.

That leads to step three for the evangelists. If evangelists encounter anyone who is superstitions, they can assure individual targets that "greater is He who is in you (or will be in you) than He who is in the world" (1 John 4:4). Jesus is greater, stronger than any superstition. Once Jesus lives in us, he protects the redeemed from any powers of darkness that come against them.

Points to Ponder

1. How was Jacob an evangelist?

2. Both Jacob and his wives were superstitious. Where do superstitions come from? How do superstitions factor into evangelism? How can superstitions get in the way of accepting Jesus?

3. Name superstitious behaviors that are a part of 21st century life that an evangelist may have to deal with in targets of evangelism.

4. What was the significance of God changing Jacob's name to Israel? Compare and contrast Jacob's behavior before and after his name change?

5. Compare and contrast the behavior of an individual before and after accepting Jesus as Savior.

6. Why did Jacob bury idols/images at Shechem before traveling to Bethel? What was the significance of the idol burial?

10

JOSEPH AND ASENATH

Joseph is the fourth and final Israelite Patriarch in
Lore, Legends, Lies. In the *Bible*, Joseph was the
oldest son of Rachel and Jacob, but the eleventh-born
son of Jacob. Jacob named Joseph "heir" and treated
Joseph better than he treated other sons. This
favorable treatment caused much of the heartache that
subsequently occurred in Joseph's life. The *Bible*
contains little information on Joseph's wife; her name
was Asenath. Legends supply information on Asenath
including her origin.

In Islam, Joseph is the only son of Jacob that is
identified as a prophet. Joseph is the noblest and most
exalted of Jacob's sons.

Sold as a Slave

Jacob's preferential treatment and Joseph's clueless
behavior in relating his dreams to his brothers caused
them to be jealous of him. When Joseph was about
17, his brothers sold Joseph to Ishmaelite traders.
From 17 to approximately 30, Joseph was enslaved or
imprisoned in Egypt.

The Ishmaelite trader's caravan likely came from
Persia, India, or even southeast Asia. The caravan
contained spices, balm (*Cymbopogon citratus*), and
myrrh (*Commiphora* genus) (Genesis 37:25).

After Joseph's brothers sold him to Ishmaelites, Joseph was scared, and in emotional and physical pain. How could this happen to him? How could his brothers act in such a despicable way? How they must hate him! Perhaps, Joseph ask himself where was his father's God during these events?

The balm carried by Ishmaelite traders wasn't used to assuage Joseph's pain. Traders weren't about to use valuable balm on a slave. Likely, the traders added to Joseph's pain. The Hebrew word for myrrh is *môr* or *mows* which translates into English as "bitter" because myrrh had a bitter taste. Imagine how bitter, Joseph felt by his brother's actions. Myrrh was an appropriate symbol of Joseph's feelings.

Enslaved and Imprisoned

The *Bible* is silent about Joseph's life after being sold to Ishmaelites and prior to being sold to Potiphar; however, legends filled in some details. Initially, Ishmaelites offered Joseph for sale to Midianites. Midianites were reluctant to buy Joseph, noting he didn't have the appearance of a slave. In order to not shame his brothers by admitting that they sold him, Joseph attempted to reassured Midianites that he was truly a slave. Still, they had doubts. Rather than sell Joseph, his owners assigned him to work with a shopkeeper and left the area. They intended to decide Joseph's fate when they returned.

While Joseph was with the shop keeper, legend recorded that the shopkeeper became rich. An Egyptian woman (Potiphar's wife) saw Joseph in the shop. She became enamored with him. Potiphar's wife convinced her husband to buy Joseph, arguing that the shopkeeper became rich by having Joseph with him. If Potiphar bought Joseph, he would become richer.

Potiphar bought Joseph. While in Potiphar's household, Potiphar's wife attempted repeatedly to seduce Joseph (Genesis 39:6-20). Eventually, Potiphar's wife wrongly accused Joseph of molesting her. Because of Potiphar's wife's accusations, Joseph was imprisoned.

A similarity exists between the *Bible* record of Potiphar's wife accusing Joseph of molesting her and a 13th century BCE Egyptian story titled *Tale of Two Brothers*. On the next page is a shortened version of the Egyptian tale. Perhaps, the *Tale of Two Brothers* influenced the *Bible* story of Joseph. The tale was written earlier than the episode of Potiphar's wife attempting to seduce Joseph.

While in prison, Joseph interpreted dreams for Pharaoh's chief cupbearer and chief baker who were temporarily imprisoned (Genesis chapter 40). Joseph remained in prison until he was about 30 years old, probably at least 10 years.

Pharaoh's Dream

The *Bible* recorded that Pharaoh had a dream about reeds that distressed him (Genesis 41:1-4) Pharaoh's concern about a dream that involved Nile River reeds

Tale of Two Brothers

Ancient Egyptian Myth

An unmarried brother, Bata, lived with his brother, Anubis, and Anubis' wife.

While Anubis was away from home, his wife attempted to seduce Bata. Bata ran away.

Anubis' wife told Anubis that Bata attempted to seduce her. Initially, Anubis believed his wife and tried to kill Bata. Ra, the sun God, prevented Anubis from killing Bata.

Eventually, Anubis discovered that his wife was the initiator. Anubis killed his wife and threw her body to dogs.

was understandable for two reasons. First, after death Egyptians believed that they traveled through the underworld. They entered the Field of Reeds where class distinctions remained with Pharaoh the ruler over all life in the Field of Reeds.

Second, the Egyptian reed (*Phragmites australis*) grew in fresh and salt water and lined Nile riverbanks. Reeds were an economic asset, used as pens and to make boats, paper, containers, and houses for poor families. Possibly, Pharaoh suspected that his dream impacted the economy of Egypt.

Joseph, Vizier in Egypt

No Egyptian wisemen or astrologers could interpret Pharaoh's dream. Joseph was called from prison to interpret it. One Arab legend contends that Joseph would only interpreted the dream if he would be released from prison. Pharaoh agreed.

In the *Bible*, not only did Joseph interpreted Pharaoh's dream, but he explained how to mitigate the dream's negative effects on Egypt. Pharaoh appointed Joseph as Vizier (second in command only to himself) over Egypt.

Pharaoh arranged for Joseph to marry Asenath, daughter of the chief priest of On (Heliopolis) (Genesis 41:45, 41:50-52). Asenath birthed two sons, Manasseh (older) and Ephraim. By legend, both sons were educated with Pharaoh's sons. They were known for their wisdom. Legend claimed that Manasseh was the steward over Joseph's house.

Another Asenath <u>legend</u> recorded that Potiphar found the abandoned infant, Asenath, and took her home. Later, when Potiphar's wife accused Joseph of molesting her, Asenath spoke up and denied the wife's accusation. Asenath saved Joseph's life. Potiphar put Joseph in prison rather than killing Joseph. At the time Potiphar declared that Asenath would marry Joseph. See the scroll on the next page for another legend of how Asenath got to Egypt.

In the *Book of Mormon* Joseph, while in Egypt, saw a vision of the Nephites (2 Nephi chapter 3). Joseph prophesized about Moses who would deliver the Israelites from Egypt and of the coming of Joseph Smith and the *Book of Mormon*.

In his role as Pharaoh's second in command, Joseph sold grain during the famine. This famine wasn't localized to Egypt, but extend at least as far as Canaan. In the *Bible* Jacob's sons went from Canaan to Egypt to buy grain. Joseph met his brothers when they came to Egyptian to buy grain. Although the brothers didn't recognize Joseph, Joseph recognized them.

Approximately, 20 years passed between Joseph's brothers selling him to Ishmaelites and Joseph meeting his brothers when they came to Egypt to buy grain and other food.. In that time interval Joseph aged from a youth to a man. Joseph wore the elaborate headdress and makeup of Egyptian nobility. Both deterred his brothers from recognizing Joseph.

Asenath

Jewish Tradition

Asenath, Joseph's wife, was the daughter born to Dinah following her rape by Prince Shechem. Jacob wrote God's name and the episode on a gold plate. He placed the plate around the infant's neck.

Dinah left her infant daughter on a city wall in Egypt. An Egyptian priest walked near the wall and heard the infant's cry. He took her home. He and his wife named her Asenath and reared her as their daughter.

Eventually, the priest became the chief priest of a powerful Egyptian god. Pharaoh arranged a marriage between Joseph and Asenath to show his regard for Joseph.

This legend teaches God foresees all. God directed matters so that Joseph would have a suitable wife in Egypt.

The first time Joseph's brothers came to purchase grain (*Bible*), Joseph sold them grain; however, demanded that they return to Egypt with their youngest brother (Benjamin). Joseph kept his half-brother, Simeon, hostage to guarantee their return with Benjamin.

Have you ever wondered why Joseph kept Simeon as hostage when Joseph's brothers made their first trip to Egypt? Why not one of the other brothers, i.e., one nearer to Joseph's age? Why not Reuben the oldest son of Jacob? Israelite/Jewish sages wrote that Reuben wanted leniency for Joseph when Joseph's brothers sold him to caravan traders (Genesis 37:21). In contrast, Simeon wanted to kill Joseph. Joseph knew Simeon's murderous nature and kept Simeon in Egypt to protect Jacob's family from Simeon.

When Joseph brought Jacob and family to Egypt, they settled in Goshen, in northern Egypt. Goshen was sparsely populated and ideal for grazing flocks.

Joseph's Death

When Joseph died his body was mummified. Joseph's body was taken from Egypt in the Israelite exodus. Joseph was buried in tribal lands of Ephraim in Canaan.

The *Qur'ān*, recorded the Joseph was buried in Hebron, not in Ephraim as the *Bible* noted. According to the *Qur'ān,* Joseph was buried beside, but not inside, the cave of Machpelah. Asenath burial site wasn't given. Most likely she was buried in Egypt.

What about Evangelism?

Stripped of clothing, thrown into a cistern, sold into slavery, wrongly accused of molesting his owner's wife, imprisoned, forgot about by those he helped. If anyone had a right to be bitter and vindictive, it was Joseph.

Joseph's outstanding characteristic is that he learned from his mistakes. Initially, Joseph seemed to accept, even delight in Jacob's favoritism. Somewhere in the process of being sold as a slave, wrongly accused of molesting a high-ranking Egyptian woman, and being forgotten by two temporarily imprisoned Egyptian retainers, Joseph learned humility. When Pharaoh asked Joseph to interpret his dream, Joseph credited God for giving the interpretation (Genesis 41:16). Joseph's mindset transformed from being self-centered to God-centered.

Evangelists must be God-focused. Giving the message of Jesus, the son of God, isn't the time for self-glorification. True, God uses evangelist's words to lead an individual to Jesus, or to plant seeds in an individual. These seeds may later germinate and the individual makes the decision to accept Jesus as Redeemer. Either way, credit for an individual's salvation belongs to God.

Have you ever reported to your church group or your spouse that you "saved" an individual at work this week? Evangelists are conduits or channels from God to a person. When the individual accepts Jesus as Savior. God saves them. God gets the credit.

Despite the brother's viciousness in taking Joseph's coat, throwing him into a pit, and selling him to caravan traders, Joseph wept when he saw his brothers. He was overcome with love for them. Not nursed anger, even residual anger, but love! God can take an evangelist's suboptimal reasons for telling individuals about Jesus and use them for his glory.

About 25 years ago, I realized that my heart was hard. This was after spending time as a missionary. I was indifferent to whether or not other individuals outside my circle of family and friends were going to heaven. Now, it is hard to accept that my motives for telling other about Jesus were all wrong.

What did I do about my realization of hard-heartedness? Prayer, prayer, and more prayers for a softer heart. Remember the proverb, "Be careful what you pray for, you might get it." I got a soft heart. Somedays, my soft-heartedness is uncomfortable. Do you wonder if Joseph ever asked himself why he was saving his brothers from starvation or why he had such a soft heart toward them?

Joseph exhibited confident behavior. Confidence, not arrogance, is another trait needed in evangelism. He was confident when he interpreted Pharaoh's dream and when he gave a way to mitigate the horrendous effect of future famine in Egypt. Joseph's confidence came from belief that God gave him the right interpretation and right solution to the dream's effects. Joseph had the confidence, not in Pharaoh, nor in himself, but in God.

Evangelists can have the same confidence Joseph had. Evangelist have the written word of God that can be read and memorize (hide in our heart) to construct a message of Jesus' redemption to targeted individuals. Using Joseph as an example, evangelist can confidently relate Jesus's work of redemption to targeted individuals.

Pharaoh embraced Joseph's message and was perhaps overawed by him. Evangelists shouldn't expect that hearers will be overawed by their message. Because every targeted individual doesn't accept the evangelist's message doesn't mean that evangelist's gives up taking the messages of Jesus' salvation to lost individuals. The evangelist's role is to plant a seed. God has the responsibility for germination. Perhaps, a target will only turn to Jesus years after receiving the message of salvation. God's timeline is far different than humankind's timeline.

Points to Ponder

1. Was it consistent/inconsistent with cultural norms for Jacob to declare Joseph his heir? How may an evangelist be required to go against 21st century cultural norms?

2. If your sibling acted like Joseph's brothers acted, would you want to tell them about Jesus as Savior? Why or why not?

3. The *Bible* is relatively silent on Asenath. Which legends do you believe and which ones do you think are false about her life? What should an evangelist think and say about Asenath?

4. When you tell an individual about Jesus, what are your motives?

5. Are you confident in Jesus' redeeming work in your life? Are you confident to tell others about Jesus as Redeemer? Could a non-confident individual be an evangelist? Should a non-confident individual be an evangelist?

6. Remember the lines of the late 21st century song that went something like, 'when you moved your mouth to speak, the blood went to my feet.' When targets hear an evangelist, will they automatically become overawed by the message?

Final Thoughts

We are amazed by similarities when we compare and evaluate *Bible* episodes with those of other cultures and faiths. Some well-known theologians account for similarities in oldest human records by noting that humankind had a common origin. Humans didn't divide into smaller language-based groups until after the Tower of Babel incident.

The slogan of my church is "Relentlessly pursuit of God and the people He loves." God loves all individuals. In almost all faiths, evangelists want non-believers to embrace the Triune God, God the Father, God the Son (Jesus) and God the Holy Spirit. Evangelists' message is simple: believe in Jesus and accept Jesus as Redeemer (Acts 16:31),

It's almost impossible to convince an individual to believe in God unless you:

- Have solid ideas about what you believe.
- Have a relationship with the individual targets of your evangelism message.
- Have a well-crafted message of your beliefs that resonates to targets.

Using Genesis events and characters provided in *Lore, Legends, Lies*, evangelists got ideas for relentless pursuing people God loves.

Resources

Ali, M. M. *The Holy Qur'ān*. Columbus, Ohio: Lahore, Inc. 1995.

Barron, R. Gospel Reflections. *Word on Fire Institute*. www.wof.com.

Carnahan, W. (Translator). *The Epic of Gilgamesh*. https://www.ancienttexts.org.

Chabad.org. https://www.chabad.org.

First People, American Indian Legends. https://www.firstpeople.us.html.

Flowers in Israel. https://www.flowersinIsrael.com.

Folkard, R. *Plant Lore, Legends, and Lyrics*. Alpha editions. (2019, original publication date 1882).

Garden of Eden. *Myth and Legends*. https://www.mythencyclopedia.com.

Ginsberg, L. *Legends of the Bible*. Barnes & Noble Books. https://www.barnesandnoble.com. (1956, original publication 1909).

Hageneder, F. *The Meaning of Trees*. San Francisco, CA: Chronicle Books. 2005.

Ham, S. Is Genesis 1–11 a derivation from ancient myths? *Answers in Genesis.* https://www.answersingenesis.org.

Hamilton, V. P. *Handbook on the Pentateuch.* Grand Rapid, MI: Baker Books. 2015.

Hamori, E. J. Echo of Gilgamesh in the Jacob story. *Journal of Biblical Literature, 130*(4), 2011, 625-642.

Hareuveni, N. *Trees and Shrubs in our Biblical Heritage.* Kiryat Ono, Israel: Neot Kedumin, Ltd. 1989.

Joshua, J. M. Enuma Elish - The Babylonian Epic of Creation - Full Text. *Ancient History Encyclopedia.* https://www.ancient.eu/article/.

Jewish Women's Archives. *Sharing Stories Inspiring Change.* https://www.jwa.org.

Myths of Holy People (Book Seven). *University of Missouri.* https://www.umsl.edu.

Mytho Religio. https://www.mythoreligio.com.

Neusner, J. *The Mishnah, A New Translation.* New Haven, CT: Yale University Press. 1988.

Pai-Gang, H. *Korean Myths and Folk Legends.* https://www.abcbooks.com.

Rabinowitz, L. I. *Torah and Flora.* New York, NY: Sanhedrin Press. 977.

Reedsburg, G.A. *The book of Genesis* (videos). Chantilly, VA: The Great Courses.

Skinner, C. M. *Myths and Legends of Flowers, Trees, Fruits, and Plants*. Forgotten Books. https://www.forgottenbooks.com.

Smith, J. Junior (Translator). *The* Book of Mormon, *Another Testament of Jesus Christ*. St. Lake City: The Church of Jesus Christ of Latter-Day Saints. 1981.

Strong, J. *The New Strong's Exhaustive Concordance of the Bible*. Nashville, TN: Thomas Nelson. 2010.

Sumerian religion. *Wikipedia*. https://www.wikipedia.org.

Whiston, W. (Translator). *The Works of Josephus, Complete and Unabridged*. Peabody, MA: Hendrickson Publishers, Inc. 1987.

Whispering Books. https://www.whisperingbooks.com.

AUTHOR INFORMATION

Dr. Carolyn A. Roth

Carolyn is a spiritual woman who believes in the Trinity — God the Father, God the Son, and God the Holy Spirit. She believes that words in the *Bible* are inspired words from God. In this publication she named them "lore."

Dr. Carolyn A. Roth has advanced degrees in psychology and a doctorate from the University of San Francisco. She spent 25 years teaching in universities. Her last full-time position was as a Distinguished Professor.

Carolyn is an Ordained Minister and the author of 10 non-fiction books on the *Bible*. She is immersed in theology and science. She writes books for laity rather than clergy or theologians. Many of her books are designed as *Bible* studies.

Carolyn is eager to hear your questions and comments. Her email is carolyn.roth@ymail.com.

Made in the USA
Columbia, SC
16 October 2022

69526384R00087